EVERYONE LOVES

TACOS

EVERYONE LOVES
TACOS

BEN FORDHAM & FELIPE FUENTES CRUZ

rps

RYLAND PETERS & SMALL
LONDON • NEW YORK

To our wives, Siobhan and Kay Lee, for all that they have given and put up with as we embarked on another book. To our kids, Ferran and Yasmin; and Penelope, Beatrice and Hazel, they continue to inspire and motivate us in everything we do.

Senior Designer Megan Smith
Commissioning Editor Alice Sambrook
Picture Researcher Christina Borsi
Production Manager Gordana Simakovic
Art Director Leslie Harrington
Editorial Director Julia Charles
Publisher Cindy Richards

Food Stylist Emily Kydd
Prop Stylist Luis Peral
Indexer Vanessa Bird
Spanish Translations Dalia Garcia Aquino

First published in 2018.
This revised edition published in 2022
by Ryland Peters & Small
20–21 Jockey's Fields
London WC1R 4BW
and
341 E 116th St
New York NY 10029

www.rylandpeters.com

10 9 8 7 6 5 4 3 2

Text copyright © Ben Fordham and
Felipe Fuentes Cruz 2018, 2022
Design and commissioned photography
copyright © Ryland Peters & Small 2018, 2022

ISBN: 978-1-78879-434-3

MIX
Paper | Supporting
responsible forestry
FSC® C008047

Printed in China

A CIP record for this book is available from
the British Library.
US Library of Congress Cataloging-in-
Publication Data has been applied for.

NOTES
• For information on unusual ingredients and substitutions, refer to page 142.
• We hope that you'll be making lots of your own tortillas, however, we know that you'll sometimes need to use the store-bought variety. The standard size is about 15 cm/6 inches, so we have assumed that size for the recipes. However, if you are making them yourself you'll need to adjust the size you make accordingly.
• Whether to use flour or corn tortillas (or even mezcla, which is a combination of both) is really up to you. We generally favour corn (particularly for fish and seafood fillings), but we would certainly opt for flour at breakfast time.
• Both British (Metric) and American (Imperial plus US cups) ingredients measurements are included in these recipes for your convenience, however it is important to work with one set of measurements and not alternate between the two within a recipe.
• All spoon measurements are level unless otherwise specified.
• All eggs are medium (UK) or large (US), unless specified as large, in which case US extra-large should be used. Uncooked or partially cooked eggs should not be served to the very old, frail, young children, pregnant women or those with compromised immune systems.
• When a recipe calls for the grated zest of citrus fruit, buy unwaxed fruit and wash well before using. If you can only find treated fruit, scrub well in warm soapy water before using.
• We usually leave the seeds in our chillies/chiles but, if you prefer a milder taste, remove the seeds to tone down the heat.

PICTURE CREDITS
All photography by Peter Cassidy apart from pages:
10 left Eric Raptosh Photography/Getty Images
10 centre ©fitopardo.com/Getty Images
10-11 Stuart Westmorland/Design Pics/Getty Images
11 centre Holgs/Getty Images
11 right Margie Politzer/Getty Images

CONTENTS

ABOUT BENITO'S HAT

Felipe and I started Benito's Hat in 2008 and grew it to critical and public acclaim. We also launched a small street food pop-up, selling our famous tacos, and Felipe opened Dona Nata Mexican Kitchen in Los Cabos, Mexico. Good, simple food is at the core of all of these restaurants, where sharing is encouraged and there is certainly no standing on ceremony.

The taco is one of the pillars of Mexican cuisine and has rightly become one of the most famous dishes associated with it. It is composed of a tortilla (traditionally made from corn, but wheat may also be used), folded or rolled around a filling – and that is about as simple and delicious as it gets.

Once you've decided on the principal filling, then it is all about the garnishes and salsas and here you can mix and match the flavours to your heart's content. There are some well-established classics like pork and pineapple or lamb with avocado, but as you will see, the combinations are endless. We have included recipes for meat, fish and vegetarian tacos, plus the all-important salsas and side dishes. To complete your meal, there are even some dessert taco recipes and drinks too.

Mexican food comes in all shapes and sizes, but we have always believed that the flavours shine through best if you can have as much fun cooking it as eating it. La Familia has been something we talked about at Benito's Hat since opening, and we hope that, with this book, we can welcome you into ours.

Ben Fordham

THE HISTORY OF TACOS

There are several theories regarding the history of the taco and its origins. Some claim that it predates the Spanish arrival in Mexico in the 1500s, and while it is written that the Spanish Conquistador Hernán Cortés enjoyed a taco meal with his captains in Coyoacán in 1520, there are references to tacos in Mexico well before that. However, another theory associates the origin of the taco to the silver mining industry in the 1900s, where the dynamite used to excavate the ore was called a taco. It was given this name because the gunpowder wrapped in paper resembled the miners' lunch of meat wrapped in a tortilla.

Whatever its origins, the taco has become an integral part of the food prepared in every household in Mexico. Whichever village, town or city you visit when travelling around, you will find a taco stall, taco truck or taqueria (taco restaurant) – and in every one of those places you will find exciting regional variations. The majority of the tacos in Mexico are still made with corn tortillas, but flour tortillas have really come to dominate in the north of Mexico and the USA.

We're not going to try to list every taco here, but we thought it would be useful to give you a few broad categories to help you on your journey of taco discovery. Grilled meat tacos are known as **tacos al carbon**, stewed and slow-cooked meat ones are **tacos de guisado** or **canaste**, whilst griddle-cooked meat and vegetable tacos are **tacos a la plancha**. Furthermore, there are **tacos dorados** which use lightly fried tortillas,

taquitos or flautas which are made by putting the filling in the centre of the tortilla, rolling the tortilla into an elongated cylinder and then deep-frying the whole bundle until it is crispy. And finally, for those taco lovers who like something sweet, there are even chocolate tortillas, but more on that later.

Tacos vary considerably depending on the region of Mexico that you visit. For example, **Tacos de camaron** (grilled or fried prawns/shrimp) and **Tacos de pescado** (fish tacos) originated in Baja California. Coahuila in the north of Mexico is where a traditional vegetarian **Tacos laguneros** came from, while **Tacos al pastor** are associated with the streets of Mexico City, **Tacos de chilorio** (pork) with Sinaloa, marinated pork tacos from the Yucatan, and **Tacos de canasta** in Tlaxcala. In all these regional varieties, what links them is their simplicity. At their most traditional they are a meat, or fish or veg, and a salsa... and no more than that.

During the twentieth century, many Mexicans emigrated to the USA, bringing their traditional dishes and culinary heritage with them. The growing popularity of Mexican food brought about the invention of the hard shell taco in 1947, as the corn tortilla did not stay fresh for very long. The growth of the Mexican community in the USA resulted in a spread of the love of Mexican food, and particularly the taco (in 1962, Glen Bell opened his first Taco Bell restaurant in Downey, California) and the love of Mexican food has now spread across the world.

HOW TO MAKE CORN TORTILLAS

Here is your basic tool - the humble corn tortilla. There is nothing complicated about this recipe but if this is your first time making tortillas, you will probably get it wrong a few times before you get it right. Stick with it though, as it is just a knack that comes with practice and experience and the results will transform any taco!

Masa harina is a flour made from grinding dried field corn or maize. It is available from online suppliers if you cannot find it in your supermarket.

200 g/2 cups masa harina (fine yellow cornflour/maize)
300 ml/1¼ cups warm water
¼ teaspoon sea salt
clean plastic bag
tortilla press (optional), or a large saucepan

MAKES 10 TORTILLAS, 8 CM/ 3¼ INCHES IN DIAMETER

Put the masa harina, water and salt in a mixing bowl and mix well for 3–5 minutes until you have a smooth, pliable dough. Divide the mixture into ten equal pieces and roll into balls.

Open up a plastic bag by cutting down each side so that you have one, flat piece. Place one ball of dough in the middle of the plastic bag and place this in the middle of the open tortilla press, if using one. Fold the bag in half over the dough, close the tortilla press and push the handle down firmly to compress the dough as much as possible.

Open the tortilla press and check that the tortilla is nice and thin. Compress again if necessary. Very carefully peel back the plastic from the top of the dough, making sure the dough does not tear, then flip it over in your hand so that it is dough-side-down in your hand and gently peel back the plastic.

If you don't have a tortilla press, place a large saucepan on top of the plastic-covered dough, repeatedly pressing down firmly and evenly. Now set the pan aside and pat firmly a few times with the palm of your hand to flatten the dough even further. Gently peel off the plastic as above.

Repeat this process until you have made ten tortillas.

To cook, heat a non-stick frying pan/skillet over a medium heat (don't add any oil), then cook each tortilla for 1 minute on each side until cooked through. To keep the tortillas warm, place them on a clean kitchen towel and fold the cloth over to cover them.

A good tortilla is not too thick and not too thin. If it is too thin, it will break when trying to peel the plastic off and if it is too thick, it won't cook evenly. The best tortilla should fluff up when cooked.

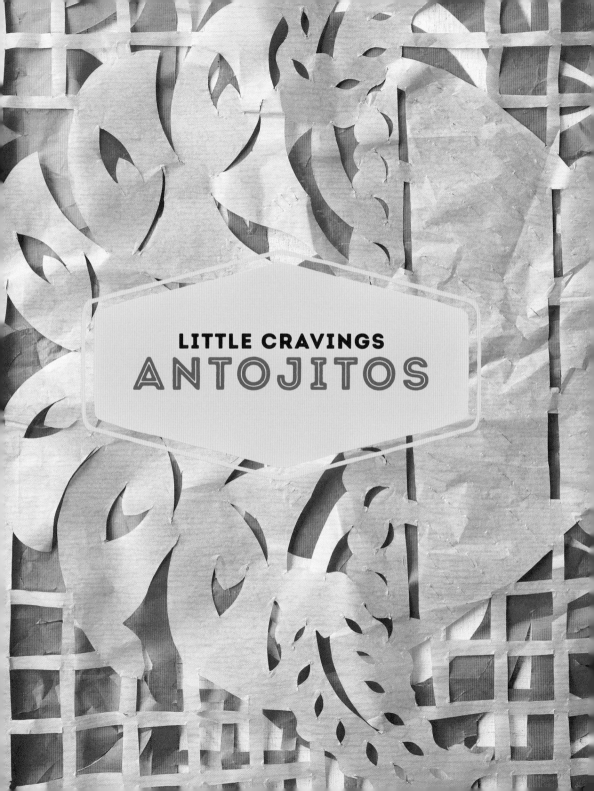

LITTLE CRAVINGS
ANTOJITOS

SHRIMP CEVICHE WITH MANGO
CEVICHE DE CAMARÓN CON MANGO

The original ceviche has a citrus flavour as it is made with limes. I have recently moved to Baja California, where mangoes are in abundance during the months of June, July and August so we have used those here. The combination of mango and lemon adds a delicious sweet and sour touch to the ceviche.

500 g/1 lb raw, shell-on
  prawns/shrimp
1 cucumber
a small bunch of fresh mint leaves
freshly squeezed juice of
  3 lemons
pulp of ½ mango
1 red Thai chilli/chile
¼ teaspoon salt
¼ teaspoon freshly ground
  black pepper
¼ red onion, thinly sliced

SERVES 4-6

Peel and clean the prawns/shrimp, removing the head, shell and black strip from each. Cut them lengthwise (but not all the way through) to make a butterfly cut.

Bring 500 ml/2 cups water to the boil in a saucepan, add the prawns/shrimp and cook for 2–3 minutes or until opaque and cooked through, then drain and place in ice to cool.

Peel and cut the cucumber in half lengthwise, remove the seeds and cut three-quarters of it into half-moons. Reserve the remaining quarter, along with the seeds, for the sauce.

Set aside 4–5 mint leaves for a garnish, then make the sauce by blending the remaining mint with the lemon juice, mango pulp, Thai chilli/chile, the remaining cucumber and the seeds, and salt and pepper.

Place the prawns/shrimp on a platter, then drizzle over the sauce and add the slices of onion and half-moons of cucumber. Put it in the refrigerator until you are ready to serve.

TO SERVE Garnish with the reserved mint leaves and serve on the platter or spoon on top of slices of toasted bread.

KING OYSTER MUSHROOM CEVICHE
CEVICHE DE HONGO OSTRA

We debated whether we could call a mushroom dish 'ceviche' but we have decided it's OK. This vegetarian version of ceviche is packed with taste and this particular mushroom is weighty enough to absorb a lot of flavour without falling apart. We've suggested you let the dish marinate for at least an hour before serving, but a little longer is better as the flavours keep on growing.

6 king oyster mushrooms
60 ml/¼ cup vegetable oil
50 g/2 cups fresh coriander/
   cilantro
3 spring onions/scallions
3 medium tomatoes
1 red chilli/chile
zest and freshly squeezed
   juice of 3 limes
a pinch of salt

SERVES 4-6

Cut the king oyster mushrooms in half, then slice them at an angle (the slices should be about 1 cm/ ½ inch thick).

In a steamer, lightly steam the cut mushrooms for about 3-4 minutes. Transfer the mushrooms to a bowl, then pour the oil over the top and allow them to cool.

Finely chop the coriander/cilantro, including the stalks. Slice the spring onions/scallions. Chop the tomatoes and the chilli/chile into small pieces.

Place the mushrooms in a large bowl, add the zest and juice of the limes, chopped coriander/cilantro, spring onions/scallions, tomatoes, chilli/chile and salt and mix well. Cover the bowl with clingfilm/plastic wrap and refrigerate for at least an hour before serving.

BEER-BATTERED AVOCADO DIPPERS
AGUACATE CAPEADO A LA CERVEZA

When it comes to using avocados in Mexican cooking, deep-frying is not what immediately springs to mind. However, this is one of those healthy/naughty treats! Take something super-healthy and then deep-fry it in a beer batter ... what's not to love? The combination of the crispy batter and the soft avocado centre is amazing, even before you dip it into the creamy chipotle mayo.

6–8 ripe avocados
vegetable oil, for deep-frying

FOR THE BATTER
165 g self-raising flour/1⅓ cups all-purpose flour mixed with 2 teaspoons baking powder
1 teaspoon salt
1 teaspoon cumin
1 teaspoon dried oregano
1½ teaspoons paprika
½ teaspoon freshly ground black pepper
1 teaspoon ground avocado leaf powder (see page 142)
1 teaspoon baking powder
1 bottle (330 ml/11 fl oz) Sol beer, or substitute your lager of choice

FOR THE CHIPOTLE MAYONNAISE
150 g/¾ cup mayonnaise
2 teaspoons chipotle paste
1 clove of garlic, peeled

SERVES 6–8

FOR THE BATTER Mix together all the dry ingredients until they are well combined. Gently stir in the beer until you have a smooth batter and then put to one side.

FOR THE CHIPOTLE MAYONNAISE Put all the ingredients in a blender and blend for about 1 minute until smooth. Set aside until ready to serve.

Cut the avocadoes in half, peel them and remove the stones. Slice each half into 3–4 pieces lengthwise, depending on their size.

Pour enough oil into a medium saucepan to reach halfway up the side and heat until hot but not smoking.

Working with one avocado at a time, dip the slices in the batter until well covered, then carefully lower into the oil – it's best to use a slotted spoon to do this to avoid spitting oil.

Fry each batch for about 1 minute so that the batter is golden coloured, but no darker, and crispy. Remove with a slotted spoon and place on a plate lined with paper towels to soak up any excess oil. Repeat with the remaining avocado slices.

TO SERVE Transfer the chipotle mayonnaise to a serving bowl and place on a large serving plate. Arrange the avocado slices on the plate, serve and watch your friends' amazement when they try this dish!

AVOCADO STUFFED WITH SHRIMP
AGUACATE RELLENO DE CAMARONES

Avocados are one of the main ingredients in Mexican cooking. The combination of avocados and prawns/shrimp is nothing new, but we are sure you will enjoy our version of it. It is light, refreshing and very easy to prepare - great as an appetizer or as a healthy snack.

200 g/7 oz/2 cups raw shell-on prawns/shrimp
½ teaspoon freshly chopped dill
a pinch of white pepper
1 tablespoon finely chopped red (bell) pepper
1 tablespoon finely chopped yellow (bell) pepper
1 tablespoon finely chopped red onion
1 tablespoon finely chopped celery
a pinch of paprika, plus extra to garnish
a pinch of salt
2 tablespoons mayonnaise
3 avocados
½ lettuce, shredded
2 limes, cut into wedges, to serve

SERVES 6

Remove the shells from the prawns/shrimp.

Place 500 ml/2 cups of water in a pan over a high heat and bring to the boil. Add the prawns/shrimp, reduce the heat to low and cook for 2–3 minutes or until opaque and cooked through. Remove from the heat, drain and allow the prawns/shrimp to cool before putting them in the refrigerator until cold.

Once cooled, cut the prawns/shrimp in half lengthwise. Place in a bowl with the dill, white pepper, chopped (bell) peppers, onion, celery, paprika and salt and mix well. Stir in the mayonnaise.

TO SERVE Cut the avocados in half and discard the stones (no need to peel the avocados).

Place the shredded lettuce in the middle of a serving plate, lay the avocados face-up and, using a spoon, fill the avocados with equal portions of the prawn/shrimp mixture. Garnish with a sprinkle of paprika and serve with the lime wedges for squeezing over.

ROASTED SPRING ONIONS
CEBOLLITAS ROSTIZADAS

My mum often served spring onions/scallions as an accompaniment to a main dish or as an appetizer on its own. The paprika adds a touch of spice and colour to the dish. The strong flavour and the texture of the charred spring onions/scallions mean that the squeeze of lime provides the perfect contrast.

**2 bunches of spring onions/
    scallions (about 16 in total)
1 tablespoon olive oil
½ teaspoon freshly ground
    black pepper
½ teaspoon paprika
1 tablespoon salt
1 lime, halved**

SERVES 4-6

Preheat the oven to 200°C (400°F) Gas 6.
    Wash the spring onions/scallions and trim the ends. Place them in a baking tray, toss with the olive oil, black pepper, paprika and salt.
    Roast in the preheated oven for 15–20 minutes, turning occasionally, until softened and lightly charred.
    Take them out of the oven and squeeze the lime over the top of them so they are well covered in juice.

TO SERVE Serve them while still nice and warm.

ROASTED CHERRY TOMATOES
TOMATITOS CHERRY ROSTIZADOS

This is an understated dish with few ingredients, but the fresh basil leaves and tomatoes work wonderfully together. Serve as an appetizer in the middle of the table and watch your guests devour them, or have it as an accompaniment to many of the dishes in this book.

1 punnet of cherry tomatoes
   (about 330 g/11 oz)
olive oil
¼ teaspoon Sal Doña Nata (see
   page 142), or sea salt
¼ teaspoon freshly ground black
   pepper
15 basil leaves, freshly chopped

SERVES 4

Preheat the oven to 200°C (400°F) Gas 6.

Place the tomatoes in a mixing bowl, add some olive oil and mix well.

Put the tomatoes on a baking tray, sprinkle the Sal Doña Nata and pepper over them and roast in the preheated oven for 15–20 minutes, until the tomatoes are soft.

TO SERVE Transfer the tomatoes to a serving platter and sprinkle with chopped basil leaves.

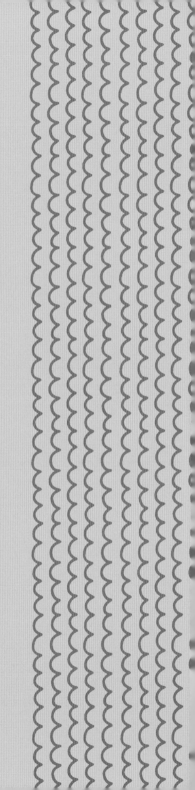

BREAKFAST & BRUNCH
DESAYUNO

MEXICAN-STYLE EGG TACOS
TACOS DE HUEVOS
A LA MEXICANA

This is Mexican-style scrambled eggs, feauring the vibrant colours of the Mexican flag. This recipe's use of simple, fresh ingredients creates a classic fusion of flavours that is very characteristic of Mexican cuisine.

6 eggs
2 tablespoons vegetable oil
¼ onion, finely chopped
1 large tomato, finely chopped
4 teaspoons finely chopped
** coriander/cilantro**
2 serrano chillies/chiles,
** deseeded and finely chopped**
1 teaspoon salt

SERVE WITH
6–8 flour or corn tortillas,
** warmed (see page 12)**
Habanero & Red Onion Salsa
** (see page 109)**
Guacamole (see page 102)

SERVES 3-4

Break the eggs into a bowl and whisk for about 30 seconds.

Heat the oil in a saucepan, then sauté the onion, tomato, coriander/cilantro, chillies/chiles and salt for a few seconds.

Add the eggs and cook over a low-medium heat for about 1-2 minutes, stirring slowly, until creamy.

TO SERVE While the eggs are cooking, heat the tortillas. Serve on the table with the eggs and salsas and let everyone help themselves.

For those who like spicy food, we have suggested serving with the Habanero & Red Onion Salsa, but the Roasted Tomatillo Salsa (see page 109) also works well with eggs and is a lot gentler on your tastebuds.

EGGS & HAM TACOS
TACOS DE HUEVOS Y JAMÓN

Most Mexican households start their day with a breakfast of eggs. There are endless combinations and here we set out another simple one. As with many such recipes, it is the combination of creamy eggs with a zesty salsa that provides the perfect balance for the morning. Having salsa with breakfast doesn't mean it has to be spicy - we have suggested the gentle Salsa Verde (Roasted Tomatillo Salsa).

6 eggs
2 tablespoons vegetable oil
125 g/4½ oz (6-8 thin slices) ham,
    chopped into pieces
1 teaspoon salt

SERVE WITH
Roasted Tomatillo Salsa (see
    page 109)
8-12 flour or corn tortillas,
    warmed (see page 12)
100 g/1 cup grated/shredded
    cheese (ideally Monterey Jack
    or mild Cheddar)

SERVES 3-4

Break the eggs into a bowl, add 1 tablespoon of the Roasted Tomatillo Salsa and whisk for about 30 seconds.
    Heat the oil in a saucepan over a low-medium heat, then add the chopped ham and the salt and sauté for a few seconds. Add the beaten eggs and cook them for about 1-2 minutes, stirring gently.

TO SERVE While the eggs are cooking, heat the tortillas. Place the warmed tortillas on the table together with the eggs, a bowl of Roasted Tomatillo Salsa and the grated cheese, and let everyone help themselves.

ALL-DAY NEW POTATO TACOS
TACOS DE PAPAS NUEVAS

Here they are in the breakfast category but, as the name suggests, these
provide a great addition to any meal whatever the time of day. Ignore the
tortillas and they become a great side to every Mexican dish. The chilli/chile
is optional but even if spice isn't your thing, I would certainly recommend
just a tiny bit to give it a little edge.

500 g/1 lb 2 oz new potatoes
2 tablespoons vegetable oil
½ red onion, finely chopped
3 tablespoons finely chopped
  parsley
1 red chilli/chile, deseeded and
  thinly sliced or finely chopped
  (optional)
a pinch of white pepper
1 teaspoon salt

SERVE WITH
8–12 flour or corn tortillas,
  warmed (see page 12)
125 g/4½ oz Cheddar cheese, cut
  into cubes
2 fresh avocados, peeled, stoned
  and diced or cut into strips
Roasted Cherry Tomatoes (see
  page 27)

SERVES 4

Place the potatoes in a saucepan with 1.5 litres/6 cups
of boiling water and boil for 15 minutes. Remove from
the heat, drain the potatoes and allow them to cool.

Cut the potatoes in half, then cut each half into
thin slices.

Put a saucepan over a high heat, add the oil and,
when hot, add the cooked sliced potatoes. Fry gently
for 2–3 minutes until they start to colour.

Add the red onion, parsley, chilli/chile (if using),
white pepper and salt and sauté them for 1 minute.

TO SERVE Heap on top of the tortillas and garnish with
small cubes of Cheddar cheese, the avocado and
Roasted Cherry Tomatoes.

PINTO BEAN & CHORIZO TACOS
TACOS DE FRIJOLES PINTOS Y CHORIZO

Pinto beans are a staple of Mexican cooking and a great source of high-quality fibre and protein. You will be hard pushed to find any restaurant in Mexico that will not serve its own version of this classic. Our recipe, which is one of the core ingredients of our burritos at Benito's Hat, uses paprika to add flavour and colour, and then we have pepped it up with the addition of some sliced chorizo.

175 g/1 cup dried pinto beans
1 tablespoon vegetable oil
150 g/5 oz chorizo, chopped
   or sliced
¼ onion, finely chopped
1 small clove of garlic, finely
   chopped
2 teaspoons paprika
½ teaspoon salt

SERVE WITH
8–12 corn or flour tortillas,
   warmed (see page 12)
200 g/7 oz queso fresco or feta
   cheese, crumbled (optional)
freshly chopped coriander/
   cilantro (optional)
150 g/5 oz chorizo, sliced
Toasted Chile de Árbol Salsa
   (see page 110)

SERVES 4

Soak the pinto beans overnight in plenty of cold water to soften them. After soaking, drain them and put into a deep saucepan with 1.5 litres/6 cups of fresh water.

Bring to the boil and boil rapidly for 10 minutes, then turn the heat down to low and cook for 2–2½ hours. Put a lid on the saucepan but do not cover fully – just tilt the lid so that there is a gap to allow steam to escape. Keep an eye on it just in case you need to add a little more water. At the end, you should be able to crush the beans easily between your fingers – but please don't try this when they are hot! If they still have some bite, cook for a little longer, adding more water if necessary.

TO REFRY THE BEANS Heat the oil in a medium saucepan, add the chorizo pieces, onion and garlic and sweat for about 1 minute.

Add the cooked beans and the paprika and cook for 10 minutes over a medium-low heat, using a potato masher to mash the beans continuously. The beans and chorizo should not be runny. Add the salt to taste.

TO SERVE Fill the warmed tortillas with the refried bean and chorizo mixture and stack next to each other on a serving plate. Now sprinkle the cheese and coriander/cilantro, if using, onto each taco and serve with the additional chorizo and salsa alongside.

BLT TACOS
TACOS DE TOCINO, JITOMATE Y LECHUGA

The taco part of this recipe is as simple as it gets, but the combination of crispy bacon with the fresh cucumber salsa is what makes this truly spectacular. To make this even fresher and healthier, we have swapped out the traditional tortillas and are using the 'L' part of the 'BLT' as the wrap. Think light lunch on a hot, summer's day, or refreshing appetizer before a bbq feast.

2 teaspoons vegetable oil
8 rashers/slices of bacon
1 Romaine lettuce
2 tomatoes, chopped

SERVE WITH
Cucumber, Aguachile & Red
**   Onion Salsa (see page 114)**
1 tablespoon freshly chopped
**   parsley**

SERVES 3-4

Place the vegetable oil in a frying pan/skillet over a medium-high heat and fry the bacon for about 6–7 minutes. Turn the bacon over several times.
   Put the bacon on a plate lined with paper towels to absorb any excess oil.
   Wash the lettuce leaves and remove the stems.

TO SERVE Take a leaf of lettuce and place it in a bowl shape on a plate. Put a rasher/slice or two of bacon in the middle of the leaf, top with some tomato and spoon over the Cucumber, Aguachile & Red Onion Salsa. Scatter over the parsley.

BURGER TACOS
TACOS DE HAMBURGUESA

This burger recipe is one of my children's favourite dishes. Putting some vegetables in the meat sneaks a bit more nutrition into their diet and the mint gives them something a bit special. These burgers have become very popular at extended family gatherings.

500 g/1 lb 2 oz minced/ground beef
½ yellow (bell) pepper, finely chopped
½ red (bell) pepper, finely chopped
2 cloves of garlic, finely chopped
¼ red onion, finely chopped
½ courgette/zucchini, finely chopped
10 fresh mint leaves, finely chopped
½ teaspoon salt
½ teaspoon freshly ground black pepper
¼ teaspoon ground cumin

CHIPOTLE KETCHUP
600 ml/2½ cups tomato ketchup
1 tablespoon freshly chopped ginger
1 tablespoon chopped chipotle chilli/chile

SERVE WITH
8 slices of Cheddar cheese
8 flour or corn tortillas, warmed (see page 12)
8 Romaine lettuce leaves
1 tomato, thinly sliced
1 red onion, thinly sliced

SERVES 4

First make the chipotle ketchup. Place all the ingredients in a blender with 90 ml/6 tablespoons water and blend for 1–2 minutes. Refrigerate until you are ready to use.

Place the minced/ground beef, (bell) peppers, garlic, onion, courgette/zucchini, mint, salt, pepper and cumin in a mixing bowl and mix together well.

Divide the mixture into four equal portions and form a burger with each one.

Cook them in a griddle pan or frying pan/skillet for 3–4 minutes on each side, turning occasionally to ensure the meat is cooked through.

When cooked, remove from the heat and cut each burger horizontally in half and top each with a slice of Cheddar cheese. (We've left the burgers whole because they look great that way, but they are a bit easier for children to eat if you cut each burger in half and spread it over two tacos.)

TO SERVE Place a tortilla on a plate, layer on a lettuce leaf, then the burger with cheese, and top with tomato and red onion. Serve with the bowl of Chipotle Ketchup for people to serve themselves. Or if you wish, you can smear the ketchup over the tortillas before laying on the lettuce, burger and other toppings.

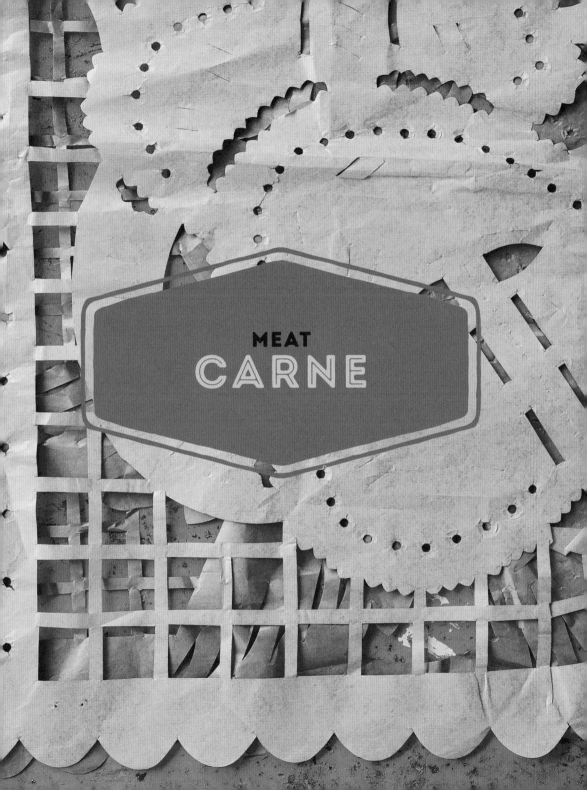

MEAT

CARNE

BEEF BRISKET BARBACOA TACOS
TACOS DE BARBACOA DE RES

Barbacoa is one of the most traditional and evocative meals of my childhood as it always meant a celebration! Often a whole sheep or goat would be used, but here we have gone for beef brisket.

100 g/3½ oz red onions
300 g/10½ oz large tomatoes
2 kg/4½ lb trimmed beef brisket
4 tablespoons paprika
2 teaspoons ground cumin
1 tablespoon chopped chipotle chilli/chile
2 teaspoons avocado leaf powder (see page 142)
3 teaspoons salt
1 teaspoon freshly ground black pepper
2 teaspoons rice vinegar

SERVE WITH
2 limes, cut into wedges
12 flour or corn tortillas, warmed (see page 12)
1 avocado, peeled, stoned and diced
Chargrilled Salsa (see page 98)

SERVES 4

Slice the red onions about 1 cm/½ inch thick. Slice the tomatoes into wedges.

Cut the beef into big chunks and place in a large lidded saucepan. Pour 2 litres/quarts water into the pan and add the onions, tomatoes, paprika, cumin, chipotle chilli/chili, avocado leaf powder, salt, black pepper and rice vinegar. Mix together with a large spoon.

Place the pan over a high heat and bring to the boil, then cover with a lid and reduce the heat to low. Simmer gently for 3 hours, stirring occasionally and making sure the pan does not boil dry.

Shred the meat inside the saucepan using tongs or a fork. Just before serving, squeeze one of the limes over the shredded meat.

TO SERVE Put the meat on a tortilla, add avocado, some Chargrilled Salsa and a squeeze of lime juice.

ROASTED PORK BELLY TACOS
TACOS DE CARNITAS

In Mexico, carnitas means 'little meats' and refers to the fact that you first slow-cook the meat, and then chop it into small pieces before crisping it up in a pan at the last minute. This method results in beautiful and tender meat that has a little bite to it. Add in the juice and zest of the orange and you have a really special, citrus-sweet flavour.

1 kg/2¼ lb pork belly
2½ teaspoons salt
2 tablespoons vegetable oil
zest and juice of 2 oranges

SERVE WITH
12 flour or corn tortillas, warmed
  (see page 12)
Pico de Gallo (see page 113)
Felipe's Chipotle Slaw (see
  page 105)
2–3 spring onions/scallions,
  thinly sliced
50 g/2 oz radishes, thinly sliced
Apple Salsa (see page 101)

SERVES 3-4

Preheat the oven to 220°C (425°F) Gas 7.

Pour 500 ml/2 cups of water into a deep roasting tray. Place a rack in the roasting tray, then place the pork on the rack to prevent it touching the bottom of the tray. Cover the pork evenly with 2 teaspoons of the salt. Cover the whole container with a lid or foil, put it in the preheated oven and cook for 1½ hours.

When the pork is cooked through, transfer to a chopping board. Discard any bones or cartilage and chop the meat into strips about 5 mm/¼ inch thick and 5 cm/2 inches long.

Heat the oil in a saucepan, add the meat and sauté for about 5 minutes to crisp up. Add the remaining salt and the orange zest and juice and continue cooking, stirring continuously, for another 5–7 minutes.

TO SERVE Place some pork in the centre of each warmed tortilla and top with Pico de Gallo, Felipe's Chipotle Slaw, spring onions/scallions, radishes and Apple Salsa.

PORK & PINEAPPLE TACOS
TACOS AL PASTOR

This is a dish from Central Mexico. Al pastor means 'in the style of the shepherd'. The tower presentation is a showstopper, but don't worry if it topples over as it will still taste great!

1 kg/2¼ lb skinless, boneless pork
    shoulder/Boston Butt, excess
    fat removed
¼–½ fresh pineapple
2 tablespoons vegetable oil

MARINADE
1–2 Guajillo chillies/chiles,
    reconstituted if dried
1–2 cloves of garlic, peeled
3 whole cloves
1 teaspoon salt
2½ teaspoons dried oregano
1 teaspoon ground cumin
1 teaspoon ground cinnamon
2½ teaspoons paprika
1 small onion, cut into pieces
1 tablespoon achiote paste
125 ml/½ cup white vinegar
zest of 1 orange
125 ml/½ cup fresh orange juice

SERVE WITH
10–12 corn or flour tortillas,
    warmed (see page 12)
onion and coriander/cilantro mix
    (see page 51)
2 whole limes
Tropical Pineapple Salsa (see
    page 101)

3–5 wooden or metal skewers
    (if using wooden, soak in water
    before using)

SERVES 3–4

Cut the pork into slices about 1 cm/½ inch thick and place in a dish.

Place the marinade ingredients in a blender. Peel 100 g/3½ oz of the pineapple and cut into pieces. Add to the blender and blend for 2–3 minutes or until smooth.

Place the oil in a saucepan over a medium heat, pour in the marinade and cook gently for 3–5 minutes, stirring. Pour the marinade over the meat, coating all the slices well, then cover the dish with clingfilm/plastic wrap and leave to marinate for at least 4 hours (or ideally overnight in the fridge).

Preheat the oven to 180°C (350°F) Gas 4. Remove the oven shelves, leaving one on the bottom runner, as you need plenty of headroom.

Peel and thickly slice the remaining pineapple (do not remove the core) and place one slice in the middle of a roasting tray.

This is the tricky bit and you may need some help. Professionals have a thick pole-like wooden skewer they place through the centre to build the 'pastor tower', but you may need to use several wooden or metal skewers. The photo shows what you are aiming for but don't worry if you end up using lots of skewers – the key is to keep it standing!

Put a long skewer through the middle of the core of the thick slice of pineapple and layer the meat slices on top, starting with the widest slices at the bottom, medium slices in the middle and the smallest at the top. The idea is that it resembles a pork-and-pineapple Christmas tree! When all the meat is on the skewer, top with the remaining slice of peeled pineapple and wrap the end of the skewer (if using wooden) in foil. Brush any of the remaining marinade over the outside of the tower.

Roast the meat in the preheated oven for 1½ hours (the internal temperature should reach at least 75°C/167°F). It should char a little on the outside and these crispy bits are the ones you give to your favourite person! If it is becoming too charred during cooking, cover with foil.

TO SERVE Bring your tower to the table with a flourish! Slice the meat from the edge, including the pineapple, as if carving a joint, then return any of the meat you don't use to the oven to char the outside a bit more. It may fall apart now but don't worry. Place the meat and pineapple on the tortillas, sprinkle on the onion and coriander/cilantro mix, squeeze over some lime juice and cover the meat with Tropical Pineapple Salsa.

BEEF TONGUE TACOS
TACOS DE LENGUA DE RES

Don't be put off by the idea of beef tongue (Ben was for a long time and only rarely let me put it on the menu!). It is like more common cuts of meat, but a bit fattier and milder than most. Boiling and softening it first is essential to avoid it becoming tough, but when prepared properly, it has a luxurious softness to it. Beef tongue is very common in Mexico and on the menus of even the smallest taquerias, but due to the time and care taken in preparing it, it is considered a delicacy.

1 beef tongue, approx 2 kg/4½ lb
3 dried chillies/chiles de árbol
3 dried chillies/chiles guajillo
3 cloves of garlic, peeled
½ onion
1 teaspoon salt

SERVE WITH
35 g/⅓ cup finely chopped
   coriander/cilantro
½ onion, finely chopped
Guacamole (see page 102)
2 limes
12-16 flour or corn tortillas,
   warmed (see page 12)

SERVES 4

Cut the beef tongue into 4-5 pieces.

Break the chillies/chiles into 3-4 pieces, crush the garlic and slice the onion.

Place the beef tongue in a medium saucepan, add the chillies/chiles, garlic, onion, salt and 2 litres/quarts of water. Cover with a lid. Bring to the boil over a high heat, then reduce the heat to low and simmer gently for 3 hours or until the tongue is tender and a knife goes into it easily. It has to be super tender for the best flavour. If necessary, top up the water during cooking to prevent the pan boiling dry.

Meanwhile, mix together the coriander/cilantro and onion, make the guacamole, slice the limes into wedges and put to one side.

Take the cooked beef tongue out of the saucepan and discard the skin, which should peel off easily using tongs and a fork. If it does not, then it could probably do with a little extra cooking time. Chop the beef into small pieces and put in a serving bowl. Keep covered so that it stays nice and warm.

TO SERVE Place a warm tortilla on a plate, add some beef tongue pieces, sprinkle over some of the coriander/cilantro and onion mix, squeeze lime juice on top and serve with a spoonful of the Guacamole.

GREEN MEATBALL TACOS
TACOS DE ALBÓNDIGAS VERDES

This recipe is a take on a classic taco called Taco de Guisado. The mix of mint, coriander/cilantro and chillies/chiles brings a wonderful herby flavour to the meatballs, so try this mixture the next time you make them to go with pasta.

500 g/1 lb 2 oz minced/ground beef
½ onion, finely chopped
3 cloves of garlic, finely chopped
3 teaspoons finely chopped mint leaves
1 teaspoon white pepper
1 teaspoon salt
40 g/⅔ cup dried breadcrumbs
2 tablespoons vegetable oil
400 g/14 oz tomatillos (tinned/canned or fresh)
1 tablespoon finely chopped coriander/cilantro
1 green Thai chilli/chile, stem removed

SERVE WITH
rice
8–10 flour or corn tortillas, warmed (see page 12)
Avocado & Radish Salsa (see page 102)
Lime & Red Onion (see page 106)

SERVES 3–4

Place the beef, onion, garlic, 1 teaspoon of the mint, a third of the white pepper, a third of the salt and the breadcrumbs in a bowl and mix together well.

Divide the beef mixture into 14 pieces, each weighing about 30 g/1 oz. Roll each piece into a ball and set aside.

Now is a good time to cook your rice. You may have your own way, and the time will depend on the type of rice you are using. The quantity you cook will depend on how many people you are feeding. I like to heat a little olive oil in a saucepan, add the rice and stir for a minute, then pour in the right amount of cold water (generally about double the volume of rice), cover, bring to the boil, then simmer until done (try not to lift the lid and mess with it during the simmering). A good squeeze of lime is a great finishing touch.

Heat the vegetable oil in a large frying pan/skillet and brown the meatballs evenly on all sides for 2–3 minutes. Lift out the meatballs with a slotted spoon, set aside on a plate lined with paper towels to soak up excess oil and wipe out the pan.

Put the tomatillos, coriander/cilantro, Thai chilli/chile and the remaining mint, white pepper and salt in a blender. Blend for about 1 minute.

Pour the mixture from the blender into the frying pan/skillet and sauté for 1–2 minutes, then add the cooked meatballs and 500 ml/2 cups of water. Bring to the boil, then reduce the heat, cover and simmer for 7 minutes.

TO SERVE Place the warmed tortillas on a plate and top with the meatballs. Serve with a bowl of Avocado & Radish Salsa, Lime & Red Onion and the rice and dig in.

SPINACH, CHORIZO & POTATO TACOS
TACOS DE CHORIZO CON PAPAS Y ESPINACAS

My children love potato tacos and, in this recipe, I even managed to sneak some spinach in there and they still love it. The chorizo adds a touch of spice and great colour to the potatoes and spinach.

100 g/3½ oz chorizo
1 medium potato
1 red onion
2 tablespoons vegetable oil
100 g/2 cups baby spinach leaves
a pinch of salt
a pinch of white pepper

SERVE WITH
a bunch of watercress
100 g/3½ oz radishes, thinly
  sliced
5-6 corn or flour tortillas,
  warmed (see page 12)
200 g/1½ cups crumbled queso
  fresco or feta cheese
Smoked Chipotle Salsa (see
  page 98)

SERVES 2-3

Cut the chorizo into slices about 5 mm/¼ inch thick.
  Peel the potato and cut it into small strips. Thinly slice the red onion.
  Heat the oil in a saucepan over a medium heat, add the chorizo slices and cook for 2 minutes. Then add the potato strips and fry for 6-8 minutes until cooked. Add the onion, spinach, salt and white pepper and cook for another 1-2 minutes, then put them to one side.

TO SERVE Place the watercress and radish slices in two separate bowls on the table. Place the chorizo mixture in the middle of the warmed tortillas and add the crumbled cheese. Add a dollop of salsa and serve.

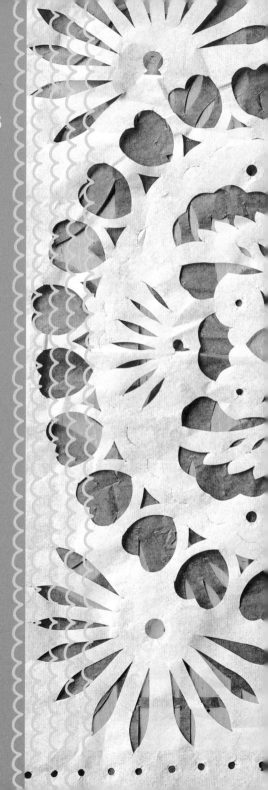

CHICKEN TINGA TACOS
TACOS DE TINGA DE POLLO

Chicken Tinga orginates in my home state of Puebla. This is a one-pot (albeit used several times) versatile dish of shredded chicken that is quick and easy to make. The tinga sauce should be a rich, earthy red and is given a good punch by the chipotle chillies/chiles.

500 g/1 lb 2 oz skinless,
   boneless chicken breasts
1 large onion, chopped
3 tomatoes, cut into wedges
2 cloves of garlic, peeled
2 tablespoons chipotle paste
¾ teaspoon white pepper
1 tablespoon paprika
1½ teaspoons salt
2 tablespoons vegetable oil

SERVE WITH
12 flour or corn tortillas, warmed
   (see page 12)
½ romaine lettuce, shredded
1 bunch of radishes, sliced
½ red onion, sliced
150 ml/⅔ cup sour/soured cream
200 g/7 oz feta cheese, crumbled

SERVES 3-4

Place the chicken in a small saucepan with 1 litre/quart of water, bring to the boil, then simmer for 10 minutes. Skim the froth from the top if necessary.

Remove the saucepan from the heat. Remove the chicken from the pan and put to one side to cool. Pour the broth into a separate bowl and reserve for later. When the chicken is cool enough to handle, shred into small pieces.

In the now-empty saucepan, place 20 g/¼ cup of the chopped onion, the tomatoes and garlic and 500 ml/2 cups water, bring to the boil, then simmer for 5 minutes. Drain, discard the water and leave to cool.

Once cooled, place in a blender with the chipotle paste, white pepper, paprika and salt and blend for 1 minute until completely smooth.

Take the saucepan again and heat the oil, then add the remaining chopped onion. Sauté for 1 minute, then add the shredded chicken and the mixture from the blender and cook for another minute. Add 125 ml/½ cup of the reserved chicken broth and simmer over a low heat for 15 minutes.

TO SERVE Place a generous spoonful of chicken tinga on top of each warmed tortilla. Top up with the lettuce, radishes, red onion, sour/soured cream and finally the crumbled feta cheese.

LAMB SHANK BIRRIA TACOS
TACOS DE BIRRIA DE BORREGO

This was the dish that Ben said made him fall in love with my cooking so, if not for this, Benito's Hat may never have happened. Birria is a spicy stew from the central Mexican state of Jalisco. It is traditionally made with lamb or goat, but beef or chicken can also be used. This popular dish is often made for special celebrations, such as weddings and baptisms.

4 small lamb shanks, each weighing approx. 350 g/12 oz
15 g/½ oz dried Guajillo chillies/chiles, seeds and stems removed
2 cloves of garlic, peeled
1 onion, chopped
300 g/10½ oz tomatoes, cut into wedges

MARINADE
25 g/1 oz fresh ginger, peeled
1 tablespoon dried oregano
1 teaspoon ground cumin
1 teaspoon ground cinnamon
3 tablespoons paprika
1 teaspoon freshly ground black pepper
1 tablespoon salt
2 whole cloves
2 tablespoons white vinegar

SERVE WITH
12 flour or corn tortillas, warmed (see page 12)
Onion, Coriander/Cilantro & Radish Salsa (see page 110)
Toasted Chile de Árbol Salsa (see page 110)
2 limes, cut into wedges

SERVES 4

Preheat the oven to 140°C (275°F) Gas 1.

Put the lamb shanks into a large roasting pan and set aside for a moment.

Put the chillies/chiles, garlic, onion and tomatoes into a saucepan. Add 1.5 litres/quarts of water, bring to the boil and simmer for 5 minutes. Drain, discard the water, and set aside to cool.

Put all the marinade ingredients into a blender and blend. Then add the cooled chillies/chiles, garlic, onion and tomatoes and blend until you have a smooth purée.

Pour the mixture from the blender onto the lamb and spread over evenly, massaging it in with your hands. Cover the dish completely with foil, doubling-up to ensure there are no gaps. Cook in the middle of the preheated oven for 3–3½ hours until very tender. Check occasionally and baste by spooning some of the marinade from the base of the pan over the lamb. The lamb should pull away easily with a little pressure from a fork – if it doesn't, cook for a little longer.

TO SERVE Pull the meat from the bones and shred, discarding the bones and fat. Tent the meat with foil to keep it warm.

Place the warmed tortillas in a stack on the table together with a bowl of the Onion, Coriander/Cilantro & Radish Salsa, the Toasted Chile de Árbol Salsa and lime wedges and invite everyone to dig in.

ROASTED LAMB SHOULDER TACOS
TACOS DE BARBACOA DE BORREGO

Another popular dish from my home state of Puebla is Lamb Barbacoa, and my father's favourite. The slow cooking of the lamb results in a meat that is bursting with flavour as the gradual cooking allows the avocado leaves to penetrate the meat and produce a delicious consommé to accompany it. When cooked to perfection, the juicy, tender meat falls off the bone.

1½ tablespoons ground avocado leaf powder (see page 142)
2 teaspoons salt
1 kg/2¼ lb bone-in lamb shoulder

SERVE WITH
Avocado Salsa (see page 113)
Spicy Black Beans (see Salmon & Spicy Black Bean on page 66 but omit the chile de árbol)
½ onion, finely chopped
20 g/1 cup freshly chopped coriander/cilantro
1 lime
6–8 corn or flour tortillas, warmed (see page 12)

SERVES 3–4

Preheat the oven to 180°C (350°F) Gas 4.

In a large bowl, mix 60 ml/¼ cup of water with the avocado leaf powder and salt. Place the lamb shoulder into the bowl and coat with the avocado leaf mixture.

Place a roasting rack over a medium roasting tray, place the meat on the middle of the rack and spoon over any remaining avocado leaf mixture. Pour 115 ml/½ cup of water into the bottom of the roasting tray.

Cover the lamb with foil. It is best to double-up to ensure that there are no gaps at the edges of the tray. Place in the preheated oven and cook for 2½ hours.

While the lamb is cooking, prepare the Avocado Salsa and Spicy Black Beans. Mix the chopped onion and coriander/cilantro together in a small bowl. Cut the lime into 8 segments and place in a bowl.

When the lamb is cooked and tender, remove from the oven. Leave to rest and cool a little for 10 minutes, then remove the meat from the bone (this should happen very easily), discarding any excess fat. Shred the meat.

TO SERVE Add a spoonful of the Spicy Black Beans to each warmed tortilla, then add the lamb. Spoon over the Avocado Salsa and sprinkle over lime juice and the onion-coriander/cilantro mix.

CHICKEN TAQUITOS
TAQUITOS DE POLLO

Taquito (also known as a flauta) in Spanish means 'little taco'. They are tacos filled with various ingredients, rolled like a cigar, then fried until crisp. These chicken taquitos are very popular with children. They can be made using corn or flour tortillas, although corn is more traditional. Cheese is another good addition to the filling and, for a vegetarian option, herby mashed potato is a popular alternative.

2 boneless, skinless chicken
  breasts
2 cloves of garlic, crushed
¼ onion, chopped
¼ teaspoon salt
12 corn tortillas
vegetable oil, for frying

SERVE WITH
½ romaine lettuce, shredded
Pico de Gallo (see page 113)
125 ml/½ cup sour/soured cream
200 g/7 oz queso fresco or feta
  cheese

36 cocktail sticks/toothpicks

SERVES 3-4

Pour 1 litre/quart of water into a saucepan and bring to the boil. Add the chicken, garlic, onion and salt and simmer for 7-8 minutes or until the chicken is completely cooked.

Lift out the chicken and set aside to cool. Reserve the onion and garlic, and discard the cooking liquid.

Shred the cooled chicken and mix with the cooked onion and garlic.

Take one tortilla and heat in a dry, non-stick frying pan/skillet until softened and flexible.

Spoon a little shredded chicken onto the warmed tortilla, just slightly to the side of centre. Roll the tortilla into a cylinder and secure it with 3 cocktail sticks/toothpicks, gently pushing them through the cylinder. Repeat with all the remaining tortillas and chicken.

Pour vegetable oil into a deep frying pan/skillet to a depth of approx 2 cm/¾ inch. Heat over a medium heat until the oil is hot but not smoking.

Carefully drop in the taquitos in batches of 3-4 and fry for 12 minutes until golden, turning gently and occasionally to prevent them from burning.

Using tongs or a slotted spoon, remove the taquitos from the pan and allow to drain on paper towels. When the taquitos are cool enough to handle, remove the cocktail sticks/toothpicks.

TO SERVE Put a little shredded lettuce on each plate, add 3-4 taquitos, top with Pico de Gallo, sour/soured cream and crumbled cheese.

FISH & SEAFOOD
PESCADOS Y MARISCOS

SALMON & SPICY BLACK BEAN TACOS

TACOS DE SALMÓN
CON FRIJOLES NEGROS
PICANTES

A deliciously different fish taco which combines succulent oven-baked salmon
with satisfying mashed black beans, and pepped up with ginger and garlic.

BEANS
165 g/1 cup dried black beans
3 tablespoons vegetable oil
1–2 dried chillies/chiles de árbol,
    cut into small pieces
¼ onion, finely chopped
1 clove of garlic, chopped
½ teaspoon salt
1 tablespoon ground avocado
    leaf powder (see page 142)

SALMON
a splash of olive oil
500 g/1 lb 2 oz fresh salmon
    fillets, skin removed
½ teaspoon finely grated fresh
    ginger
a pinch of white pepper
2–3 cloves of garlic, finely
    chopped

SERVE WITH
12 flour or corn tortillas, warmed
    (see page 12)
Lime & Red Onion (see page 106)
fresh jalapeños, seeds and stems
    removed, thinly sliced

SERVES 4

FOR THE BEANS Put the dried beans in a deep saucepan
with 2 litres/quarts of water and bring to the boil. Turn
the heat down to low, partially cover and simmer gently
for 2 hours. Check every 30 minutes to be sure there is
still enough water and stir so that the beans don't stick
to the bottom of the pan.

After 2 hours, heat the oil in a large saucepan over a
medium heat. Add the dried chilli/chile de árbol, onion,
garlic, salt and ground avocado leaf powder and fry
gently for 15–20 seconds. Mix together with the cooked
black beans Transfer the beans and cooking water to
a blender and blend for 1 minute. Tip into a saucepan
and bring them back to simmer over a medium heat for
2–3 minutes as this will bring out the rich and aromatic
flavour. Put to one side to cool.

FOR THE SALMON Preheat the oven to 220°C (425°F)
Gas 7. Line an ovenproof dish with foil and add a splash
of olive oil. Place the salmon on the foil. Add the grated
ginger and white pepper and scatter over the chopped
garlic, gently pushing it into the fillets. Bake in the
preheated oven for 20–25 minutes.

TO SERVE Once cooked, gently break the salmon into
bite-sized pieces, about 2–3 cm/1 inch square. Layer up
the spicy beans over the warm tortillas, then add pieces
of cooked salmon and top it up with the Lime & Red
Onion and sliced jalapeños.

LOBSTER & CRAB FRITTER TACOS
TACOS DE ALBÓNDIGAS DE LANGOSTA Y CANGREJO

At Benito's Hat, we pride ourselves on being adventurous when creating new fillings for our restaurant. We developed this recipe during one particularly creative session, combining lobster and crab in a fish 'meatball', and the customers loved it! Lobster is a special occasion food, but this recipe doesn't demand too much and the flavour comes through very well.

125 g/4½ oz/1 cup lobster meat

125 g/4½ oz/1 loosely packed cup white crabmeat

3 tablespoons finely chopped parsley

2 cloves of garlic, finely chopped

½ red onion, finely chopped

½ teaspoon salt

3½ tablespoons freshly squeezed lime juice

50 g/heaping ⅓ cup plain/ all-purpose flour

500 ml/2 cups vegetable oil

SERVE WITH

sautéed courgette/zucchini slices

6 corn or flour tortillas, warmed (see page 12)

Felipe's Chipotle Slaw (see page 105)

Pico de Gallo (see page 113)

SERVES 2-3

Chop the lobster and crabmeat into small pieces and put into a large bowl. Add the parsley, garlic, red onion and salt, then stir the mixture together. Add the lime juice and flour and mix again.

Form the mixture into small balls about 25 g/1 oz each, flatten each ball slightly, and arrange them on a sheet of baking parchment as you make them.

Pour the vegetable oil into a frying pan/skillet and heat, then when hot, fry the fritters in batches for 2 minutes, turning occasionally until golden. Drain the fritters on paper towels and repeat until you have fried them all.

SAUTÉED COURGETTE/ZUCCHINI Slice a courgette/zucchini into thin strips using a peeler, and sauté in a pan with a splash of vegetable oil for 1 minute.

TO SERVE Place the warmed tortillas on a plate, add a layer of Felipe's Chipotle Slaw, lay three fritters on top, followed by the Pico de Gallo salsa and finally the sautéed courgette/zucchini slices.

OCTOPUS & PARSLEY TACOS

TACOS DE PULPO ASADO

There is a bit of work involved with preparing these tacos, but they are well
worth it. Boiling and then charring the octopus really brings out the best in
it. These tacos combine tender cooked octopus with a parsley and garlic sauce
which give it a wonderful flavour. They will provoke many 'ooohs' and 'aaahs'
at a party and the octopus can be cooked 24 hours in advance.

750 g–1 kg/1½–2¼ lb cleaned
    octopus
1 bay leaf
10 black peppercorns
1 teaspoon salt, plus extra to taste
1 head/bulb of garlic, cut in half
    around its centre
2 lemons
2 tablespoons extra virgin
    olive oil
freshly ground black pepper
2 tablespoons finely chopped
    parsley
1 tablespoon finely chopped garlic

SERVE WITH
12 corn or flour tortillas, warmed
    (see page 12)
Cucumber, Aguachile & Red
    Onion Salsa (see page 114)

12 wooden skewers

SERVES 4

Combine the octopus, bay leaf, peppercorns, salt, garlic
head/bulb and 1 lemon, cut in half, in a saucepan along
with enough water to cover. Turn the heat to medium,
cover and bring to the boil. Once boiling, reduce
the heat so that it simmers slowly and cook until the
octopus is tender, about 45–60 minutes.

While the octopus is cooking, soak the wooden
skewers in water for 5–10 minutes and set aside.

When the octopus is ready, it should cut easily
with a sharp knife. Drain, discarding everything but the
octopus, and set aside. You can prepare up to this stage
24 hours in advance and keep in the refrigerator.

Preheat the grill/broiler to medium-high. Cut the
octopus into 2.5 x 2.5-cm/1 x 1-inch pieces, then thread
them evenly onto the skewers.

Mix together the olive oil, pepper, chopped parsley
and chopped garlic and brush this mixture evenly over
the octopus. Place under the grill/broiler briefly, turning
once, until the outsides brown but the insides are not
dried out.

TO SERVE Cut the remaining lemon into wedges. Place
the tortillas on a serving platter with a heap of the
octopus skewers, the lemon wedges and the Cucumber,
Aguachile & Red Onion Salsa. One skewer is about right
per taco (but don't forget to remove the actual skewer!).

STORE CUPBOARD CHIPOTLE TUNA TACOS
TACOS DE ATÚN CON CHIPOTLE

Once you get the hang of them, taco shells are relatively easy to make and are a particularly good way of getting kids to try new things. This chipotle tuna recipe makes a great filling for the crunchy taco shells, and can be put together from items you often already have in your store cupboard (you can tweak the recipe depending on what you have available, and that goes for the Jicama & Carrot Slaw too).

½ red (bell) pepper
½ yellow (bell) pepper
1 tomato
½ bunch of spring onions/
   scallions
⅓ medium romaine lettuce
240-g/9-oz can of tuna, drained
75 g/½ cup sweetcorn/corn,
   drained
1 tablespoon chipotle paste
3 tablespoons finely chopped
   coriander/cilantro
100 g/½ cup mayonnaise
700 ml/2⅔ cups vegetable oil

SERVE WITH
8 corn tortillas (see page 12)
Jicama & Carrot Slaw (see
   page 117)

SERVES 3-4

Deseed and cut the red and yellow (bell) peppers into small chunks and dice the tomato. Thinly slice the spring onions/scallions and the romaine lettuce.

Place the vegetables in a bowl with the tuna, sweetcorn/corn, chipotle paste, coriander/cilantro and mayonnaise, and mix well.

Heat the oil in a large, deep frying pan/skillet over a medium-high heat. Carefully fold a tortilla in half, using tongs to keep it folded. Place it in the oil for a few seconds, starting with the bottom part (the fold) and then lay it on one side and then the other, frying until golden brown all over.

Remove the tortilla from the oil and drain on paper towels, then repeat with the remaining tortillas.

TO SERVE Place the taco shells on a serving plate. Fill with the tuna mix and top with the Jicama & Carrot Slaw.

DEEP-FRIED FRESH TUNA TACOS
TACOS DORADOS DE ATÚN

This spectacular taco works as an appetizer as well as a main. You cook the tuna inside the tortilla, so be sure to secure the taco well before cooking to prevent it falling apart. The flavour of the tuna and the bite of the radish salsa are beautiful.

2 tomatoes, cut into wedges

1 fresh jalapeño, stem and seeds removed

½ onion, finely chopped

2 tablespoons freshly chopped coriander/cilantro

½ teaspoon salt

300 g/10½ oz fresh tuna steak, skin removed

100 g/2 cups chopped red cabbage (about ½ a small cabbage)

a pinch of freshly ground black pepper

vegetable oil, for frying

SERVE WITH

10 corn tortillas (see page 12)

Onion, Coriander/Cilantro & Radish Salsa (see page 110)

1 fresh avocado, peeled, stoned and diced

200 g/7 oz queso fresco or feta cheese, cut into cubes

30 cocktail sticks/toothpicks

SERVES 4

Place 475 ml/2 cups of water in a small saucepan with the tomatoes and jalapeño and bring to the boil. Turn down the heat and simmer for 4–5 minutes, then remove from the heat and allow to cool.

Once cooled, drain and place the tomatoes and jalapeño in a blender with half the onion, half the coriander/cilantro and ¼ teaspoon of the salt and blend for 45–60 seconds. Put aside until ready to serve.

Chop the fresh tuna into small chunks and put in a bowl. Add the remaining onion, half the cabbage, the remaining salt and the black pepper and mix well.

In a dry, non-stick frying pan/skillet, warm the tortillas so that they are flexible.

Place a tortilla on a flat surface, add one-tenth of the tuna mixture on one side and fold the other side on top. Secure the folded-over tortilla with three cocktail sticks/ toothpicks around the edge, pushed through at an angle to ensure it doesn't break up during cooking. Repeat with the remaining tortillas and tuna mix.

Pour enough vegetable oil to reach a depth of about 2 cm/¾ inch in a frying pan/skillet. Heat the oil until very hot, but not smoking, then reduce the heat to medium.

Deep-fry the tacos in batches of 2–3 at a time for 3–5 minutes or until crispy, using metal tongs to turn them occasionally.

Remove from the heat and lay them on paper towels to soak up any excess oil. When cool enough to handle, remove the cocktail sticks/toothpicks and top each one with some Onion, Coriander/Cilantro & Radish Salsa.

TO SERVE Place 2–3 tacos on each plate, drizzle over the blended salsa and then sprinkle with the remaining chopped cabbage, coriander/cilantro, diced avocado and queso fresco or feta cheese.

SPICY SHRIMP TACOS
TACOS DE CAMARONES PICANTES

This is a favourite dish with my family as we love seafood. It is really pretty simple and there are no overpowering flavours due to the way the prawns/shrimp are cooked, but it is the combination with onion, coriander/cilantro and avocado salsa that makes this special. If you like a bit more heat, it is easy to adjust the spiciness by adding a little more crushed chilli/chile.

350 g/12 oz medium raw shell-on prawns/shrimp
1 yellow (bell) pepper
1 red (bell) pepper
50 g/3½ tablespoons butter
1 small onion, halved and then thinly sliced
4 cloves of garlic, very finely chopped
1 teaspoon crushed dried chillies/chiles
a pinch of salt
2 teaspoons finely chopped parsley

SERVE WITH
50 g/½ cup finely chopped onion
35 g/⅔ cup finely chopped coriander/cilantro
Avocado Salsa (see page 113)
12–16 flour or corn tortillas (see page 12)
2 limes, cut into wedges

SERVES 6-8

Peel the tails off the prawns/shrimp, leaving the rest of them whole.

Cut the (bell) peppers in half and discard the stems, seeds and white ribs. Cut the flesh into 2 x 3-cm/¾ x 1¼-inch pieces.

To make the onion-coriander/cilantro mix for serving, place the chopped onion and herbs in a serving bowl and mix together. Tip the Avocado Salsa into another serving bowl.

Start to warm the tortillas now as you want to be serving this dish with the prawns/shrimp piping hot.

Whilst heating the tortillas, put the butter in a saucepan and melt over a medium heat. Add the sliced onion, garlic, (bell) peppers, dried chillies/chiles and salt and cook for 4–5 minutes until soft.

Add the prawns/shrimp to the pan and cook for another 2 minutes, stirring, until the prawns/shrimp are pink and cooked through.

TO SERVE Stir in the parsley and serve immediately with the warmed tortillas, the bowl of onion-coriander/cilantro mix and the Avocado Salsa, and squeeze the lime juice over.

VEGETARIAN

VEGETARIANOS

DEEP-FRIED AVOCADO TACOS
TACOS DE AGUACATE CAPEADO

You may have noticed these 'gussied-up' avocado slices on page 20 of the Antojitos section, but here we give them the full taco treatment. The crispy-on-the-outside/creamy-soft-in-the-centre avocado wedges combine beautifully with the spicy Chipotle Slaw, fresh Pico de Gallo, sharp squeeze of lime juice and the tart crunch of fresh radishes. A mouthwatering dish if ever there was one.

2 avocados
135 g self-raising flour/1 cup
   all-purpose flour mixed with
   2 teaspoons baking powder
1 teaspoon ground avocado leaf
   powder (see page 142)
2½ teaspoons ground cumin
4 teaspoons dried oregano
3 teaspoons paprika
½ teaspoon white pepper
½ teaspoon salt
1 bottle (330 ml/11 oz) Sol beer
   (or similar crisp lager)
vegetable oil, for frying

SERVE WITH
6 flour or corn tortillas, warmed
   (see page 12)
Felipe's Chipotle Slaw (see
   page 105)
Pico de Gallo (see page 113)
2 limes, each cut into 4 wedges
thinly sliced radishes

MAKES 6

Cut the avocados in half, remove the stones and peel off the skin. Slice each half lengthwise into 3–4 slices, depending on the size of your avocados.

Put the flour into a large bowl. Add the avocado powder, cumin, oregano, paprika, pepper and salt and mix together well. Make a well in the centre, add the beer and mix gently until you have a smooth batter.

Fill a small saucepan with vegetable oil to a depth of about 7–8 cm/2¾–3¼ inches and place over a medium-high heat, or heat a deep fat fryer to 180°C/350°F.

Coat the avocado slices in the batter, then carefully lower them into the hot oil and deep-fry for 30 seconds on each side until puffy and crisp, taking care not to burn them. Fry a few slices at a time.

Remove the slices from the oil with a slotted spoon and place on a plate lined with paper towels to absorb any excess oil.

TO SERVE Layer up the warmed tortillas with the avocado fritters, Felipe's Chipotle Slaw, Pico de Gallo and a squeeze of lime juice, and garnish with thinly sliced radishes. Serve with additional slaw and the remaining lime wedges.

SPICY WILD MUSHROOM TACOS
TACOS DE HONGOS SILVESTRES PICANTES

Ben went on a foraging trip and came back with all sorts of extravagantly named mushrooms (black trumpets, chanterelles, hedgehogs, etc.) and so we had a lot of fun with those. You can be as adventurous as you like with this delicious, spicy mix of sautéed wild mushrooms, butter, fresh garlic, fresh ginger, pepper and a touch of heat.

125 g/4½ oz fresh, mixed wild or shiitake mushrooms
125 g/4½ oz button mushrooms
½ small red (bell) pepper
½ small yellow (bell) pepper
¼ onion
1 large clove of garlic, very finely chopped
15 g/½ oz fresh ginger, very finely chopped
2 teaspoons finely chopped parsley (leaves only)
1½ teaspoons crushed dried chillies/chiles
1 teaspoon salt
30 g/¼ stick butter

SERVE WITH
8-10 flour or corn tortillas, warmed (see page 12)
mixed spring leaves, such as watercress, spinach and rocket/arugula
Pico de Gallo (see page 113)
oil and vinegar salad dressing (optional)

SERVES 4

Wash the mushrooms and slice them 1 cm/½ inch thick. Cut the red and yellow (bell) pepper halves and discard the stems, seeds and white ribs. Cut into pieces about 3 cm/1¼ inches square. Slice the onion into strips about 1 cm/½ in thick.

Place the prepared vegetables in a bowl, add the garlic, ginger, parsley, dried chillies/chiles and salt and stir to mix well.

Put a saucepan over a high heat and melt the butter for about 1 minute. Then add the mushroom mixture, stir together and sauté for 6-8 minutes.

TO SERVE Place a warm tortilla on a plate, add a layer of mixed leaves, followed by a small spoonful of Pico de Gallo and top with a generous spoonful of the wild mushrooms. Serve with additional mixed leaves and a simple oil and vinegar dressing, if you wish.

SAUTÉED ASPARAGUS TACOS
TACOS DE ESPÁRRAGOS A LA PLANCHA

As surprising as it may seem, my children love asparagus and so I wanted to create a dish using their favourite veg. This simple mix highlights the delicate flavours of the vegetables and balances it with the creamy, tartness of the feta cheese for a dish full of colour and flavour.

500 g/1 lb 2 oz asparagus
1 courgette/zucchini
1 red (bell) pepper
1 yellow (bell) pepper
60 ml/¼ cup vegetable oil
¼ red onion, sliced
a pinch of salt
a pinch of freshly ground
　black pepper
2 cloves of garlic, finely chopped
1 dried chile de arbol, finely
　chopped
2 tablespoons finely chopped
　parsley

SERVE WITH
12 flour or corn tortillas, warmed
　(see page 12)
Salsa Fresca (see page 106)
feta cheese, crumbled

SERVES 4–5

Cut off and discard the woody bottom ends of the asparagus spears.

Cut the courgette/zucchini in half lengthways, discarding the ends. Slice each half into half-moons about 5 mm/¼ inch thick.

Cut the (bell) peppers in half and discard the stems, white ribs and the seeds, then slice into strips.

Add the oil to a frying pan/skillet, bring it to a high heat and sauté the asparagus for 2–3 minutes. Add the onion, courgette/zucchini, (bell) peppers, salt and pepper to the pan and continue to sauté for another 3 minutes. Finally, stir in the garlic, chile de árbol and parsley and stir continuously for another 1–2 minutes.

TO SERVE Pile the filling in the middle of the warmed tortillas, add the Salsa Fresca and sprinkle some feta cheese on top.

TURMERIC & POTATO TACOS
TACOS DE PAPA CON CÚRCUMA

Having read about the health benefits of turmeric, we wanted to add it to a recipe that we cook on a regular basis. It turns the potatoes a pretty vibrant colour but don't let that put you off as they taste fantastic and my children, in particular, are huge fans of this dish.

500 g/1 lb 2 oz potatoes, peeled and chopped into small pieces
1–2 whole fresh jalapeño chillies/chiles
3 tablespoons vegetable oil
1 red onion, finely chopped
2 cloves of garlic, chopped
½ teaspoon ground turmeric
¼ teaspoon dried oregano
2 teaspoons salt

SERVE WITH
12 flour or corn tortillas, warmed (see page 12)
Red Cabbage Mix (see page 105)
Pico de Gallo (see page 113)
100 g/3½ oz Cheddar cheese, cubed

SERVES 4-6

Place the chopped potatoes in a saucepan of boiling water and boil for 8-10 minutes until tender. When the potatoes are cooked, drain them and set aside.

Cut the jalapeño chillies/chiles in half, remove the seeds and thinly slice.

Place 2 tablespoons of the oil in a frying pan/skillet over a medium heat. Add the onion, garlic and jalapeño slices and sauté for 1 minute. Next add the cooked potatoes and sauté for 5-6 minutes.

Add the turmeric, oregano and salt and continue cooking for another 2-3 minutes, gently stirring with a spoon.

Finally, add the rest of the oil and cook the mixture for another minute, before removing from the heat and placing on the side, ready to serve.

TO SERVE Spread the potato mixture in the middle of the warmed tortillas. Top them with the Red Cabbage Mix, Pico de Gallo and the cubed Cheddar cheese.

SPICY LENTIL TACOS
TACOS DE LENTEJAS PICANTES

As with many other ingredients, lentils came to Mexico via the Spanish and they can now be found in every market in the land, having become a much-used, and much-loved, staple. They absorb the aromatic spices so well and here we have gone for cumin, paprika and oregano.

200 g/1 cup uncooked green lentils, washed and drained
2 tablespoons vegetable oil
1 large onion, diced
4 cloves of garlic, finely chopped
1 fresh jalapeño chilli/chile, diced
200 ml/scant 1 cup vegetable stock
75 g/½ cup sweetcorn/corn
2 teaspoons paprika
¼ teaspoon ground cumin
¼ teaspoon freshly ground black pepper
1 teaspoon dried oregano
1 teaspoon salt

SERVE WITH
10 corn tortillas (see page 12)
12 cherry tomatoes, roughly chopped
½ head cos lettuce, thinly sliced
½ jicama/yam bean, peeled and grated
Guacamole (see page 102) or diced avocado
Beetroot/Beet Salsa (see page 114)

SERVES 4

Preheat the oven to 180°C (350°F) Gas 4.

Put 600 ml/2½ cups of water in a saucepan, add the lentils and bring to the boil over a high heat. Reduce the heat to low, cover and simmer for about 20 minutes until the lentils soften. Drain and set aside.

Heat the oil in a saucepan and sauté the onion, garlic and jalapeño for 2–3 minutes over a medium heat, stirring frequently, until the onion starts to turn brown and translucent.

Add the cooked lentils, vegetable stock, sweetcorn/corn, paprika, cumin, black pepper, oregano and salt and bring to the boil. Reduce the heat to low, cover and simmer for 5–7 minutes, stirring frequently and adding more water, 1–2 tablespoons at a time, as needed, to stop the vegetables sticking to the pan.

Drape each corn tortilla over two bars of a horizontal oven shelf so that the tortilla's two opposing sides hang down evenly, facing each other. Bake the tortillas for 5–7 minutes until crisp.

Remove the tortillas from the oven shelf and admire your new taco shells.

TO SERVE Spoon the lentil mixture into the taco shells and top with the tomatoes, lettuce, jicama/yam bean, Guacamole and Beetroot/Beet Salsa.

NOTE For a lighter alternative, use romaine lettuce leaves as a wrap instead of the taco shells.

CAULIFLOWER & CHICKPEA TACOS
TACOS DE GARBANZOS Y COLIFLOR

The combination of cauliflower and chickpeas/garbanzo beans makes a healthy taco. These are easy to make, full of protein, taste great and the presentation of them looks pretty special too!

1 red onion, chopped
2 cloves of garlic, chopped
1 teaspoon paprika
½ teaspoon ground cumin
½ teaspoon Sal Doña Nata (see page 142), or sea salt
½ teaspoon dried oregano
1 tablespoon olive oil
1 small cauliflower
1 carrot
250 g/1½ cups canned chickpeas/garbanzo beans, drained

SERVE WITH
50 g/½ cup finely chopped onion
35 g/⅗ cup finely chopped coriander/cilantro
12–16 flour or corn tortillas, warmed (see page 12)
Avocado Salsa (see page 113)
6 radishes, thinly sliced

baking tray, greased

SERVES 6

Preheat the oven to 200°C (400°F) Gas 6.

Place the red onion and garlic in a medium bowl with the paprika, ground cumin, Sal Doña Nata, oregano, oil and 2 tablespoons of water and mix well.

Remove the leaves from the cauliflower and cut it into small florets.

Peel the carrot and remove the ends. Cut the carrot in half lengthwise, then cut each half in two again. Slice into pieces that resemble small cubes.

Put the chickpeas/garbanzo beans, cauliflower and carrot into the mixing bowl and stir the mixture to make sure the vegetables are covered with the seasoning.

Spread out the mixture on the greased baking tray and roast in the preheated oven for 35–40 minutes until the cauliflower is tender.

TO SERVE Mix the chopped onion and coriander/cilantro together in a bowl. Place a generous spoonful of the cauliflower mixture on each warmed tortilla and serve with the onion-coriander/cilantro mix, the Avocado Salsa and sliced radishes.

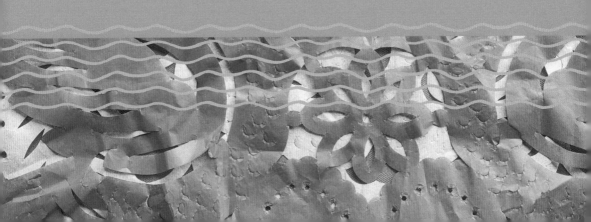

POBLANO CHILLI STRIP TACOS
TACOS DE RAJAS POBLANAS

Rajas in Spanish means 'strips', and this dish is designed to showcase the soft, smokey flavour of the poblano pepper. The poblano chillies/chiles are sliced and cooked with onions, sweetcorn/corn and cream, and you can find versions of this dish all over Mexico. However, as poblanos are not always easy to find, feel free to use (bell) peppers, but when you do find some ripe poblanos, jump at the chance to use them and you will add a whole new dimension to this dish.

4 poblano chillies/chiles
2 tablespoons vegetable oil
15 g/1 tablespoon butter
1 onion, sliced
150 g/¾ cup sweetcorn/corn
a pinch of salt
a pinch of white pepper
125 ml/½ cup sour/soured cream
125 g/1½ cups grated/shredded
  Manchego cheese

SERVE WITH
olive oil
Red Chunky Salsa (see page 106)
12 flour or corn tortillas, warmed
  (see page 12)
7-8 radishes, thinly sliced
100-150 g/¾-1 cup feta cheese,
  crumbled
freshly chopped coriander/
  cilantro

SERVES 4-6

Roast the chillies/chiles over the flame of the stove, using tongs, until the skin has evenly burned. Place them in a clean plastic bag, wrap the bag in a towel and let them rest until they have cooled.

Then, using a paper towel, peel the skin from the chillies/chiles (you can also put the chillies/chiles in a bowl of warm water to help peel off the skin). Slice open the chillies/chiles, discard the stems and seeds and slice into long, thin strips.

Heat the oil and butter in a saucepan over a medium heat and sauté the onion until transparent, then add the chilli/chile slices and sweetcorn/corn. Season with the salt and white pepper and cook for 3-5 minutes.

Reduce the heat and add the sour/soured cream and Manchego cheese. Stir to melt the cheese, then turn off the heat immediately and serve.

TO SERVE Add a splash of olive oil to the Red Chunky Salsa before serving. Add a spoonful of creamy poblana strips to the centre of each warmed tortilla, sprinkle on the sliced radishes, then the Red Chunky Salsa and crumbled feta, and finally garnish with chopped coriander/cilantro.

ROASTED PUMPKIN TACOS
TACOS DE CALABAZA ROSTIZADA

Pumpkins are a versatile and a very underused ingredient that can work equally well in savoury and sweet dishes. They are abundant in autumn but if not available, butternut squash can be used as a very able substitute. The crunchiness of the dressing adds a wonderful contrast to the smooth consistency of the pumpkin.

1 kg/2¼ lb fresh pumpkin
4 tablespoons olive oil
1 teaspoon salt
1 teaspoon freshly ground black
  pepper
1 teaspoon ground cumin
1 teaspoon ground avocado leaf
  powder
1 teaspoon chilli/chili powder
½ red (bell) pepper
½ yellow (bell) pepper
¼ red onion
2 cloves of garlic, peeled
75 g/½ cup sweetcorn/corn

SERVE WITH
10-12 corn or flour
 tortillas, warmed (see page 12)
Beetroot/Beet Salsa (see
  page 114)
Toasted Pumpkin Seeds (see
  page 117)

SERVES 4-5

Preheat the oven to 220°C (425°F) Gas 7 and place a roasting tray in it to heat up.

Peel the pumpkin, discard the seeds, and cut the flesh into small cubes.

Place the cubed pumpkin in a large bowl and add 2 tablespoons of the olive oil, and half of the following ingredients: salt, pepper, cumin, ground avocado leaf powder and chilli/chili powder. Mix well, making sure that all the pumpkin pieces are thoroughly coated.

Scatter the mixture on the preheated roasting tray. Bake in the preheated oven for about 20-25 minutes or until the pumpkin is soft and charred at the edges.

Cut the red and yellow (bell) peppers in half and discard the stems, seeds and white ribs. Cut the (bell) peppers into small pieces.

Chop the onion and garlic and mix with the (bell) peppers. Add the sweetcorn/corn and the remaining olive oil, salt, pepper, cumin, ground avocado leaf powder and chilli/chili powder and mix well. Add to the roasting tray of pumpkin, stir well and bake for another 15-20 minutes. Stir it a few times during baking to be sure it is evenly roasted.

TO SERVE Put a good spoonful of the cooked pumpkin mixture in the middle of each warmed tortilla and serve with the Beetroot/Beet Salsa and the Toasted Pumpkin Seeds.

SALSAS, RELISHES & SIDES
SALSAS Y GUARNICIONES

CHARGRILLED SALSA
SALSA TATEMADA

A great example of a salsa that would work equally well as a dip or a sauce. Charring the ingredients gives a light, smoky flavour.

250 g/9 oz tomatoes
100 g/3½ oz tomatillos (fresh if possible, but tinned/canned can also be used)
250 g/9 oz large onion
2–3 cloves of garlic, peeled
2 tablespoons olive oil
10 g/⅓ oz dried chilli/chile de árbol, stem removed
a pinch of salt, or to taste

SERVES 6-8

If using tinned/canned tomatillos, leave them out of these first stages and simply add them in at the blender stage.

Preheat the grill/broiler to a high heat.

Cut the tomatoes and fresh tomatillos in half. Cut the onion into about 4 big pieces. Place the tomatoes, fresh tomatillos, onion pieces and the cloves of garlic on a baking tray and grill/broil for about 5–10 minutes, or until they are gently charred. Set aside to cool.

Put a non-stick frying pan/skillet over a medium heat, add the olive oil and sauté the chilli/chile de árbol for about 30 seconds. Then add 60 ml/¼ cup of water, remove from the heat and set aside to cool.

Put all the ingredients apart from the salt into a blender, including the tinned/canned tomatillos if using. Blend for about 30 seconds until combined but slightly chunky. Transfer to a serving bowl and add salt to taste.

SMOKED CHIPOTLE SALSA
SALSA DE CHIPOTLE

You can adjust the amount of chillies/chiles you use here to taste - this recipe is for medium-hot.

100 g/3½ oz tomatoes, cut into wedges
½ onion, cut into pieces
2½ tablespoons vegetable oil
1 tablespoon crushed dried chillies/chiles
70 g/¼ cup chipotle paste
1 tablespoon agave syrup
1 tablespoon salt
60 ml/¼ cup rice vinegar
¼ teaspoon freshly ground black pepper
¼ teaspoon ground cumin
¼ teaspoon dried oregano
½ teaspoon hickory powder

SERVES 6-8

Put the tomatoes, onion and 250 ml/1 cup of water into a saucepan, bring to the boil and simmer for 5 minutes. Drain and discard the cooking water and set the tomatoes and onion to one side.

Place the vegetable oil in a saucepan over a medium heat, add the crushed dried chillies/chiles and fry for 1–2 minutes, being very careful not to let them burn. Add the tomatoes and onion right at the end, then remove from the heat and set aside to cool.

Transfer the cooled mixture to a blender, add all the remaining ingredients and blend until smooth.

Put a saucepan over a high heat, add the mixture from the blender and bring to the boil. Boil for about 1–2 minutes, adding 60–100 ml/ ¼–⅓ cup of water if the mixture is too thick.

This salsa is best served cold so allow time for it to cool or put in the fridge before serving.

TROPICAL PINEAPPLE SALSA
SALSA DE PIÑA

This is a wonderful salsa to serve with pork or simpler vegetable dishes. The combination of sweet pineapple with very hot habaneros is spectacular but not for the faint-hearted!

2 tablespoons vegetable oil
100 g/3½ oz yellow (bell) peppers, cored, deseeded and roughly chopped
¼ onion, roughly chopped
300 g/10½ oz fresh pineapple chunks
100 g/3½ oz Scotch bonnet chillies/chiles (habaneros)
2 teaspoons salt, or more to taste
300 ml/1¼ cups rice vinegar
3½ tablespoons agave syrup

SERVES 6-8

Put the oil in a frying pan/skillet set over a medium heat, add the yellow (bell) peppers, onion and pineapple and sauté for about 15 minutes.

Remove from the heat, add 300 ml/ 1¼ cups of water and set aside to cool.

Once cool, transfer the ingredients to a blender, add the chillies/chiles, salt, rice vinegar and agave syrup and blend for about 2 minutes until smooth. Taste and add more salt if required.

Cover the salsa and keep in the refrigerator as it is best served chilled.

APPLE SALSA
SALSA DE MANZANA

A fresh and tangy salsa for lovers of apple sauce.

300 g/10½ oz Golden Delicious apples
3 tablespoons olive oil
7 g/⅙ oz. dried chilli/chile de árbol, stem removed
¼ red onion, finely chopped
1 tablespoon freshly squeezed lime juice
250 ml/1 cup unsweetened apple juice
2 teapoons salt
1½ teaspoons freshly chopped coriander/cilantro

SERVES 6-8

Peel and core the apples. Cut into quarters, then roughly chop the quarters into 5-mm/ ¼-inch squares.

Put a non-stick saucepan over a high heat, add 2 tablespoons of olive oil and sauté the apple pieces for about 10 minutes until charred and caramelized, then set aside to cool.

Set another non-stick saucepan over a medium heat. Add the remaining oil and sauté the chilli/chile de árbol for about 30 seconds, then remove with a slotted spoon and set aside. Next, add the red onion to this oil, sauté for 30 seconds, then set aside to cool.

Put the sautéed apples, lime juice, cooked chilli/chile de árbol, apple juice and salt into a blender and blend for 1 minute.

Pour the mixture from the blender into a bowl, add the sautéed red onion and fresh coriander/cilantro and mix well before serving.

AVOCADO SALSA
GUACAMOLE

Guacamole is one of the most well-known dishes, its origins dating back to the sixteenth century. The recipe varies throughout Mexico, but this is the way we like it as all the other ingredients are designed to help the flavour and texture of the avocados shine through as much as possible.

2–3 avocados
1 bunch of coriander/cilantro
a pinch of sea salt
a pinch of ground white pepper
1 tomato

SERVES 6–8

Cut the avocados in half, remove the stones and scoop the flesh out into a bowl.

Finely chop the coriander/cilantro and add to the bowl with the salt and pepper. Roughly mash with a fork.

Finely chop the tomato and stir into the guacamole.

AVOCADO & RADISH SALSA
SALSA DE AGUACATE Y RÁBANO

This dish takes some of the most used, but also contrasting, ingredients in Mexican cooking, and simply puts them together. Creamy avocado, tart radish and onion, sharp lime and a little chilli/chile heat, for a colourful, refreshing salsa.

1 large avocado
7–8 radishes
½ small onion
15 g/¼ cup coriander/cilantro
1 fresh jalapeño chilli/chile (stem removed)
freshly squeezed juice of 1 lime
¼–½ teaspoon sea salt, to taste

SERVES 6–8

Cut the avocado in half, remove the stone, scoop out the flesh and dice it.

Thinly slice the radishes. Finely chop the onion, coriander/cilantro and jalapeño.

Combine the avocado, radishes, onion, coriander/cilantro and jalapeño in a bowl and stir. Sprinkle the lime juice and salt on top and mix again.

RED CABBAGE MIX
ENSALADA DE COL MORADA

I like serving this soon after making it when the cabbage still has a very satisfying crunch, but it can be left to stew and soften in the fridge for several days. A very simple and tasty accompaniment to vegetarian and seafood dishes.

100 g/3½ oz red cabbage
1 tablespoon olive oil
2 tablespoons balsamic vinegar
a pinch of salt
a pinch of freshly ground black
   pepper

SERVES 6-8

Cut the red cabbage in half and then finely slice each half, discarding any tough stems.

Place in a bowl and add the olive oil, balsamic vinegar, salt and black pepper and mix well.

FELIPE'S CHIPOTLE SLAW
ENSALADA DE COL AL CHIPOTLE ESTILO FELIPE

Here, smoke-dried jalapeño (known as a chipotle) provides a delightful gentle heat to go with creamy mayonnaise and crunchy vegetables.

2 teaspoons chipotle paste
1 clove of garlic, peeled
150 g/¾ cup mayonnaise
125 g/4½ oz white cabbage
60 g/2½ oz red cabbage
1 carrot

SERVES 6-8

Place the chipotle paste, garlic and mayonnaise in a blender and blend together for just under 1 minute.

Slice both cabbages as finely as you can, discarding any tough stems. Place in a bowl.

Peel the carrot, chop off the ends and discard, then grate into the bowl containing the cabbage.

Mix together the carrot and cabbage, and then combine with the mayonnaise from the blender and mix well.

FRESH SALSA

SALSA FRESCA

I use a combination of boiled fresh tomatoes and canned plum tomatoes for this salsa. This was a happy accident, the result of some experimenting in our busy kitchens, but the combination works brilliantly. Just using fresh, or just tinned tomatoes simply doesn't have the same result.

1 kg/2¼ lb fresh tomatoes
250 g/9 oz tinned/canned peeled
    plum tomatoes
50 g/¼ cup finely chopped onion
10 g/¼ cup fresh Thai chillies/
    chiles, finely chopped
20 g/⅜ cup finely chopped
    coriander/cilantro
3 teaspoons salt

SERVES 6-8

Cook the whole fresh tomatoes in a saucepan of boiling water for 12–15 minutes. Drain, discarding the water, and leave the tomatoes on the side to cool.

Once cooled, remove the skins and put the tomatoes in a bowl with the tinned/canned plum tomatoes. Squash the tomatoes with your hands (it is best to wear plastic gloves for this), then remove any big pieces and finely chop with a knife before adding them back into the bowl.

Add the onion, chillies/chiles and coriander/cilantro to the bowl. Add the salt and mix very well.

RED CHUNKY SALSA

SALSA ROJA
TROCEADA

A delightful mix to serve with almost anything.

½ red (bell) pepper
¼ red onion
a splash of olive oil
1 tablespoon finely chopped
    coriander/cilantro

SERVES 6-8

Cut the (bell) pepper and onion into chunks, add a splash of olive oil and the coriander/cilantro and mix well.

LIME & RED ONION

CEBOLLA MORADA
CON LIMÓN

A delicious salsa served with fish and pork.

2 red onions
2 tablespoons vegetable oil
1 fresh jalapeño chilli/chile
2 tablespoons freshly squeezed lime juice
a pinch of dried oregano
1 teaspoon salt

SERVES 6-8

Cut the onions in half and then cut them into 5-mm/¼-in thick slices.

Put a small saucepan over a medium heat, add the oil and fry the onions and whole jalapeño for about 1 minute, stirring continuously to cook it evenly. Be careful not to let the mixture stick and overcook.

Remove the onions and jalapeño from the saucepan and put in a small bowl. Allow to cool, then add the lime juice, oregano and salt and mix well.

HABANERO & RED ONION SALSA
SALSA DE HABANERO Y CEBOLLA MORADA

This simple relish packs quite a punch. If you do not like very hot salsas, we recommend that you start out with a small amount of chilli/chile and build up to the level of heat that suits you and your family and friends.

1 habanero chilli/chile, stalks
   removed and sliced
½ red onion, sliced
freshly squeezed juice of 2 limes
a pinch of salt

SERVES 6–8

Put all the ingredients in a bowl and stir together until they are well mixed.

ROASTED TOMATILLO SALSA
SALSA VERDE

No self-respecting Mexican restaurant, or household, is without a good Salsa Verde. It goes with everything so make a big batch and never let it run out!

1–2 fresh green chillies/chiles
   (such as serrano or Thai green),
   stalks removed
2 cloves of garlic, peeled
2–3 fresh tomatillos, husks
   removed (or tinned/canned
   tomatillos)
1 teaspoon rock salt
3 tablespoons freshly chopped
   coriander/cilantro
½ onion, chopped

SERVES 6–8

Preheat the oven to 200°C (400°F) Gas 6.
   Put the chillies/chiles, garlic and fresh tomatillos on a baking sheet and roast in the preheated oven for 20 minutes or until charred. If using tinned/canned tomatillos, don't roast them, but add them at the grinding stage instead.
   Halve the chillies/chiles and scoop out and discard the seeds. Using a molcajete or pestle and mortar, pound the chillies/chiles, garlic and salt into a paste. Add the tomatillos and grind until well mixed. Add the coriander/cilantro and onion and stir with a spoon. Add a little water or extra salt, if required.

ONION, CORIANDER & RADISH SALSA

RÁBANOS CON CEBOLLA Y CILANTRO

Quick, easy and very colourful, this salsa brightens up your table and adds a crisp and refreshing bite to your tacos.

5 tablespoons finely chopped onion
2 tablespoons finely chopped coriander/cilantro
1 bunch of radishes, thinly sliced

SERVES 6-8

Put all the ingredients into a bowl and mix together well.

TOASTED CHILE DE ÁRBOL SALSA

SALSA DE CHILE DE ÁRBOL

Take care when toasting the chillies/chiles as they give off a strong aroma - I would recommend opening the windows! Don't let this put you off though - the smell will have your mouth watering.

2 dried chillies/chiles de árbol, stems removed
2 fresh tomatoes
1 clove of garlic, peeled
¼ teaspoon salt

SERVES 6-8

Place a saucepan over a medium heat, add the dried chillies/chiles de árbol and toast for about 1 minute (they should be charred on all sides and give off quite a strong smell), then set aside.

Place the tomatoes and garlic in a dry saucepan and toast them for 4–5 minutes, turning them several times to cook evenly, but keep the lid on when you are not turning them.

Put all the ingredients in a blender with the salt and blend for 1 minute, then tip into a serving bowl.

If you think the salsa is a little runny, you can thicken it by pouring it into a frying pan/skillet and simmering gently.

AVOCADO SALSA
SALSA DE AGUACATE

A medium-spicy salsa with a wonderful creamy texture, great with lamb or beef tongue tacos.

100 g/3½ oz whole green tomatillos (fresh if possible, but tinned/canned will do)
1–2 fresh green chillies/chiles (such as serrano or Thai green), stems removed
2 cloves of garlic, peeled
1 avocado
1 teaspoon freshly chopped coriander/cilantro (the thin stalks can be used, just discard the thicker ends)
1 tablespoon finely chopped onion
a pinch of salt

SERVES 6-8

Preheat the oven to 200°C (400°F) Gas 6.

Remove the husks from the fresh tomatillos. Place the whole chillies/chiles, garlic and tomatillos on a baking tray and roast in the preheated oven for 6–8 minutes until all are slightly charred on the outside. (If using tinned/canned tomatillos, there is no need to roast them, simply add them at the next stage.)

Cut the avocado in half and remove the stone. Using a spoon, scoop out the avocado flesh and put it in a blender. Add the roasted chillies/chiles, tomatillos (or tinned/canned if using) and garlic, coriander/cilantro, onion and salt and blend for 2 minutes. Up to 60 ml/¼ cup water can be added if it seems too thick. Add more salt to taste if required.

CHUNKY FRESH SALSA
PICO DE GALLO

When these fresh, simple ingredients are combined together, they produce a wonderful salsa bursting with flavour. Like other Mexican salsas, there are many variations, such as adding lime juice and fresh chillies/chiles. We like to keep it simple and without heat so that it can be enjoyed by everybody, including young kids, with almost anything.

4 tomatoes
¼ onion
¼ bunch of coriander/cilantro
¼ teaspoon sea salt

SERVES 6-8

Finely chop the tomatoes, onion and coriander/cilantro. Place in a bowl and mix well, then add the salt and mix again.

CUCUMBER, AGUACHILE & RED ONION SALSA
SALSA DE AGUACHILE CON PEPINO Y CEBOLLA MORADA

This salsa comes from the taquerias of Baja California and its crisp, freshness is designed to bring out the best in fish or seafood tacos.

1 cucumber
freshly squeezed juice of 3
   lemons
1 Thai chilli/chile
¼ teaspoon salt
¼ teaspoon freshly ground black
   pepper
¼ red onion, thinly sliced
2 tablespoons finely chopped
   coriander/cilantro

SERVES 6-8

Peel the cucumber and cut in half lengthwise, remove and save the seeds, then cut three-quarters of the cucumber into half-moons. Reserve the remaining quarter, along with the seeds, for the sauce.

Blend the lemon juice with the chilli/chile, the remaining quarter of the cucumber and seeds, salt and pepper.

Place the sliced cucumber and onion on a platter, cover with the lemon juice and chilli/chile mixture and the chopped coriander/cilantro, and mix well. Cover and put it in the refrigerator until you are ready to serve.

It can be served on top of tostadas, or with prawn/shrimp or fish tacos.

BEETROOT/BEET SALSA
SALSA MEDIA BRAVA

At Benito's Hat, the hot Salsa Brava has been a main-stay from the beginning. Here, I have added beetroot/beet for spectacular flavour and colour.

4 tomatoes
3 habaneros or Scotch Bonnet
   chillies/chiles, stalks removed
½ onion, roughly chopped
4 cloves of garlic, peeled
2 tablespoons vegetable oil
4 tablespoons crushed dried
   chillies/chiles
3 small steamed beetroot/beets,
   cut into pieces
sea salt

SERVES 6-8

Preheat the oven to 180°C (350°F) Gas 4.

Put the tomatoes, whole chillies/chiles, onion and garlic in a roasting dish and roast in the preheated oven for 15-20 minutes or until evenly blackened, turning occasionally with tongs. Remove from the oven and allow to cool for about 10 minutes.

Heat the oil in a saucepan for 1 minute. Remove the pan from the heat, add the crushed chillies/chiles and stir well, then allow to cool.

Put the cooled crushed chillies/chiles and oil in a blender with the roasted chillies/chiles, onion, garlic, beetroot/beets and a little salt and blend together thoroughly.

Add the roasted tomatoes and blend well for another 2 minutes. Add 175 ml/¾ cup of water and a couple of pinches of salt and continue to blend until the mixture is smooth.

JICAMA & CARROT SLAW
ENSALADA DE JÍCAMA Y ZANAHORIA

Jicama, also known as yam bean, is rather like a Mexican turnip. It is usually eaten raw, often just sprinkled with a little lime juice, and has become a very popular salad ingredient.

½ jicama/yam bean
1 carrot
freshly squeezed juice of 1 lime
a pinch of salt
a pinch of freshly ground black
   pepper

SERVES 6-8

Peel and grate the jicama/yam bean. Peel and grate the carrot, then combine the two in a large bowl.

Squeeze the juice of the lime over the mixture, add the salt and pepper and mix well.

TOASTED PUMPKIN SEEDS
PEPITAS TOSTADAS

These are known as pepitas, and you'll see people munching on them on every street in Mexico's bustling cities. Eat them to keep you going through the day, make them your spicy, salty go-to snack to have with a cold drink, or sprinkle them over a simple green salad.

140 g/1 cup pumpkin seeds
½ teaspoon ground paprika
¼ teaspoon salt
1 tablespoon vegetable oil

SERVES 6-8

Place a saucepan over a medium heat, add the pumpkin seeds and toast for 5-7 minutes in the dry pan until they give off a toasted aroma, stirring continuously.

Turn off the heat and add the paprika, salt and vegetable oil and mix well.

Place a paper towel on a plate and tip the pumpkin seeds onto the plate so that any excess oil can be absorbed. After a few minutes, tip the seeds into a serving bowl.

POSTRES

CHOCOLATE ICE CREAM TACOS WITH AGAVE
TORTILLA DE CHOCOLATE CON HELADO

As chocolate originates from Mexico we certainly couldn't go through the whole book without a couple of chocolate recipes. These take a bit of time and patience to make but, for chocolate lovers, they are well worth the effort.

100 g/1 cup masa harina (fine yellow cornflour/maize)
135 g/1 cup plain/all-purpose flour
30 g/¼ cup cocoa powder
½ teaspoon salt
80 ml/scant ⅓ cup olive oil
30 g/⅛ cup agave nectar or runny honey

SERVE WITH
vanilla ice cream
100 g/1 cup chopped walnuts
dulce de leche/store-bought caramel (or see below right to make your own), to decorate

SERVES 12

Preheat the oven to 200°C (400°F) Gas 6 and line a baking tray (or several trays) with greaseproof paper/baking parchment.

Place the masa harina into a large bowl. Sift in the flour and cocoa powder. Add the salt. Make a well in the centre and add the olive oil, agave nectar or honey and 200 ml/generous ¾ cup of warm water. Mix the ingredients well and knead it into a pliable dough. Split the dough into 12 equal-sized balls. Follow the instructions on page 12 to make the tortillas, with each measuring approx 8–10 cm/3¼–4 inches in diameter.

Place the tortillas on the lined baking tray and bake in the preheated oven for 6–7 minutes. You may have to bake them in batches. Remove from the oven and allow to cool.

TO SERVE Place the cooled chocolate tortillas on a plate and, using a spoon, scrape out a few strips of vanilla ice cream and place on each tortilla. Sprinkle on some chopped walnuts and drizzle over some dulce de leche.

EVER MADE YOUR OWN CARAMEL? It's really very easy. Simply take a 397 g/14 oz. can of condensed milk and place in a medium saucepan full of water. Bring to the boil and reduce the heat so that it is simmering, then cover and simmer gently for 4 hours, keeping the water topped up so that the can is always submerged. Carefully remove the can and allow to cool before opening and there you have it – homemade caramel!

BAKED TACOS WITH STRAWBERRIES, CHOCOLATE ICE CREAM & PISTACHIO
TACOS AL HORNO DE FRESAS Y HELADO DE CHOCOLATE

This is one of the most straightforward desserts, but you've got all the good stuff in there - chocolate, ice cream, fruit and salty nuts. You can always pretend that you'd been slaving away in the kitchen for hours instead of enjoying a well-earned margarita!

4 flour tortillas
150 g/1½ cups strawberries
100 g/¾ cup pistachios
4 scoops of chocolate ice cream

SERVES 2-4

Preheat the oven to 220°C (425°F) Gas 7.
    Fold the tortillas in half, place them on a baking tray on the middle shelf of the preheated oven, and bake for 10-12 minutes until crispy. Turn them over 2-3 times during the cooking and help them to open up as well as checking that they are not burning.
    Put them on one side to cool.
    Slice the strawberries. Deshell (if necessary) and roughly chop the pistachios.

TO SERVE Place each tortilla on a plate, add a generous scoop of chocolate ice cream to each, top with the sliced strawberries and then sprinkle with pistachios.

APPLE PIE TAQUITOS

TAQUITOS DE PAY DE MANZANA

This is another US-influenced dish and we hope that 'Grandma' would approve
of our version of her traditional apple pie. The mix of cinnamon and nutmeg
adds a hint of spice to the apple and, once the taquitos are baked, the crispy
tortilla package provides a great contrast.

200 g/1 cup caster or granulated
  sugar
3 teaspoons ground cinnamon
4 medium cooking apples
  (we like to use Bramleys or
  Granny Smiths)
½ teaspoon ground nutmeg
60 g/½ stick unsalted butter
12 flour tortillas
100 ml/⅓ cup agave syrup
6 scoops of vanilla ice cream
6 fresh mint leaves, to decorate

12 cocktail sticks/toothpicks

SERVES 6

Preheat the oven to 180°C (350°F) Gas 4.

Mix 3 tablespoons of the sugar and 2 teaspoons of
the cinnamon together in a bowl and set aside.

Peel, core and cut the apples into small chunks.
Place the apples, nutmeg and the remaining cinnamon
and sugar in a saucepan with 120 ml/½ cup of water.
Mix well until the apples are coated. Cover, place over
a medium heat and cook for 10–12 minutes until the
apples are soft, stirring regularly.

Melt the butter and use a little to brush a thin layer
over a shallow baking dish.

Lay a tortilla flat and put 2–3 tablespoons of the
apple pie mixture in the centre. Tightly roll it up and
secure the tortilla with a cocktail stick/toothpick.

Brush the taquito (the rolled and tooth-picked
bundle) with a little melted butter, then sprinkle over
some of the reserved sugar-cinnamon mixture.

Place the taquito in the prepared baking dish and
then repeat the process with the rest of the tortillas and
apple mixture, reserving about a quarter of the sugar-
cinnamon mix for later.

Bake in the preheated oven for about 15 minutes or
until the taquitos start to turn golden on top.

TO SERVE Remove the cocktail sticks/toothpicks and
place two taquitos on each plate. Drizzle a zig-zag of
agave syrup over the top and then spinkle over the
remaining sugar-cinnamon mix. Finally, add a scoop of
ice cream to each plate and decorate with a mint leaf.

CINNAMON TORTILLA & ICE CREAM TACOS
TACOS DE TORTILLA A LA CANELA Y HELADO

At Benito's Hat we have served buñuelos since our third week of business. This was our version of a classic dish created using what we had around the restaurant after a customer requested 'something sweet', and it has been a hit ever since. Here we have turned that idea into a taco shell and added melted chocolate to cover the edge of the shell.

160 g/1 cup chocolate chips
2 tablespoons butter
10 strawberries
3 tablespoons caster or
   granulated sugar
1 teaspoon ground cinnamon
500 ml/2 cups vegetable oil
6 flour tortillas

SERVE WITH
vanilla ice cream
chocolate syrup
whipped cream (your choice of
   freshly whipped or from a can)
fresh mint leaves, to decorate

SERVES 3-4

Half-fill a small saucepan with water and bring to a simmer. Place a heatproof bowl on the top of the saucepan so that it rests on the rim of the pan. Place the chocolate chips and butter in the bowl and melt until smooth, stirring occasionally. You may need to add 2–3 tablespoons of water if the mixture is too thick.

Discard the stems from the strawberries, roughly chop them, then place in a bowl with 1 tablespoon of the sugar and mix well.

Mix the cinnamon and remaining sugar together.

Put the oil in a medium saucepan over a high heat until hot and then fry the tortillas. Do this individually, turning over 2–3 times and, when it starts to crisp up, press down in the middle with tongs to curve the tortilla on one side so that it makes a taco shape.

Remove the tortilla from the oil and place it on paper towels to absorb the excess oil.

Sprinkle the sugar and cinnamon mixture all over and then dip the edge of the crispy tortilla into the melted chocolate so that it coats the rim of the taco.

Repeat this process for all the tortillas and then transfer them to the refrigerator.

TO SERVE Once cooled, place the cinnamon taco shells on a plate. First fill each one with a scoop of vanilla ice cream, then cover with zigzags of chocolate syrup, add the strawberry mixture, and finally the whipped cream. Decorate with a few mint leaves.

CHOCOLATE & TROPICAL FRUIT TORTILLA HATS
SOMBREROS DE TORTILLA CON FRUTA Y CHOCOLATE

There is a bit of work involved in coating the tortillas in chocolate but, once you have the hang of that, you'll quickly become addicted to these crispy chocolate tortilla shells. They can form the base of any dessert and you can dress them up or down depending on the company. Here we've gone for a tropical fruit filling, topped off with walnut pieces for a bit of extra crunch, but the possibilities are endless.

1 apple
¼ pineapple
1 kiwi
¼ gala or cantaloupe melon
8 grapes
2 tablespoons caster or
    granulated sugar
160 g/1 cup chocolate chips
2 tablespoons butter
500 ml/2 cups vegetable oil
4 flour tortillas, 15 cm/6 inches
    in diameter

SERVE WITH
whipped cream (freshly whipped
    or from the can, you choose)
3 tablespoons finely chopped
    walnuts

SERVES 4

Peel, core or deseed (as needed) and roughly chop the apple, pineapple, kiwi and melon into 2-cm/¾-inch cubes. Cut the grapes in half and remove any seeds. Place in a bowl, add the sugar and mix well.

Half-fill a small saucepan with water and bring to a simmer. Rest a heatproof bowl on the rim of the pan. Add the chocolate chips and butter to the bowl and melt until smooth, stirring occasionally. You may need to add 3–4 tablespoons of water if the mixture is too thick.

Put the oil in a medium saucepan over a high heat until hot and then fry the tortillas. Do this individually, turning over 2–3 times and, when it starts to crisp up, press down in the middle with a ladle for 30–40 seconds, so that the tortilla curves around it. Remove from the oil and place it on paper towels to absorb the excess oil.

Dip the crispy, hat-shaped tortilla in the melted chocolate using tongs to make sure it is covered all over with the melted chocolate. Place it on a tray. Repeat the same process for all the tortillas, then place them in the refrigerator to cool.

TO SERVE Put a chocolate tortilla hat on each plate, fill with the fruit mixture, then top with whipped cream and a sprinkle of walnut pieces.

CHIA & CINNAMON PANCAKE TAQUITOS
HOTCAKES DE CHÍA Y CANELA

It is probably the US influence, but pancakes have become a popular dish in many restaurants throughout Mexico. Here we have added chia seeds as they taste great, add a crunchy texture and are crazily good for you. Served with strawberries and cream and decorated with mint leaves, this dessert looks and tastes awesome.

200 g/1⅔ cups plain/all-purpose flour
1 tablespoon baking powder
40 g/¼ cup chia seeds
1 teaspoon ground cinnamon
2 tablespoons caster or granulated sugar
a pinch of salt
2 eggs
2 teaspoons vanilla essence
250 ml/1 cup milk
15 g/1 tablespoon softened butter, plus extra for frying

SERVE WITH
fresh whipped cream
100 g/3½ oz strawberries
2 bananas
agave nectar or maple syrup
a handful of fresh mint leaves

SERVES 4-6

Put all the dry ingredients in a mixing bowl and combine well. Put all the wet ingredients in a separate bowl and use a whisk to mix well.

Add the wet ingredients to the dry ones and ensure that all the ingredients are well combined to make a smooth batter.

Now is a good time to whip the cream to medium-firm peaks and set aside in the refrigerator. Roughly chop the strawberries, discarding the stems. Peel and slice the bananas.

Place a non-stick frying pan/skillet over a low heat, add a little knob of butter and, once melted, place 4 tablespoons/¼ cup of the batter mixture into the pan and rotate the pan so that the mixture spreads to make a pancake about 10 cm/4 inches in diameter.

Cook for 2-2½ minutes, flipping the pancake over after 1 minute of cooking, until it is brown on both sides. Repeat, using up all the batter (the mixture will make 10-14 pancakes). Stack the pancakes on a baking sheet, interleaving them with baking/greaseproof paper and keeping them warm in a low oven at 80°C (175°F) Gas ¼ until you are ready to serve.

TO SERVE Lay a tortilla on a plate, place some bananas and strawberries in the centre, spoon on a dollop of whipped cream, followed by a splash of agave nectar or maple syrup, and finally some mint leaves to decorate.

DRINKS
BEBIDAS

TOMMY'S MARGARITA
MARGARITA DE TOMMY

The story of this variation on the classic margarita is that it was invented by a legend of the tequila world, Julio Bermejo, at Tommy's Mexican Restaurant in San Francisco. It removes the orange liquor element (whether that's triple sec, Cointreau, Grand Marnier or even orange juice) and compensates with a little more tequila and agave for a purer drink. As the flavour of the tequila comes through more, it is worth using a premium tequila if possible. We take this purity one level further by using Sal Doña Nata, the salt mined by my mum, but we'll let you off if you use the more readily available Maldon variety.

lime wedge
Sal Doña Nata (see page 142) or
  Maldon sea salt
50 ml/3½ tablespoons 100% Blue
  Agave Reposado Tequila
25 ml/1½ tablespoons freshly
  squeezed lime juice
25 ml/1½ tablespoons mixed
  agave syrup (a 75:25 mix of
  agave syrup and water, to make
  pouring easier)

SERVES 1

Rim a margarita glass with the salt by first running the lime wedge around the rim and then placing the glass upside down on a saucer of the salt, leaving a light covering around the edge of the glass.

Put all the ingredients in a shaker and shake hard with a generous scoop of ice. Strain over fresh ice into the prepared glass.

To garnish, cut a small knick in the lime wedge and slide onto the rim of the glass.

SPICY GREEN MARGARITA
VERDITA MARGARITA

This margarita is nothing short of spectacular but - and this is a big but - you have got to like a little heat. A tropical, herby, citrusy, spicy margarita that slips down all too easily.

lime wedge
sea salt
8 mint leaves, plus a sprig to
  garnish
10 fresh coriander/cilantro leaves
a tiny piece of habanero chilli/
  chile
15 ml/1 tablespoon mixed agave
  syrup (a 75:25 mix of agave
  syrup and water, to make
  pouring easier)
35 ml/⅛ cup 100% Blue Agave
  Tequila Blanco
25 ml/1½ tablespoons pineapple
  juice
25 ml/1½ tablespoons freshly
  squeezed lime juice

SERVES 1

Rim a margarita glass with the salt by first running the lime wedge around the rim and then placing the glass upside down on a saucer of the salt, leaving a light covering around the edge of the glass.

Muddle together the mint, coriander/cilantro, chilli/chile and a splash of the agave mix in a shaker. Combine with all the remaining ingredients and shake hard with a scoop of ice.

Strain through a sieve into the glass. Garnish with a mint sprig.

This also makes a great virgin version (agua fresca). Simply replace the tequila with apple juice and then top up with fizzy water in a long glass.

RHUBARB MARGARITA
MARGARITA DE RUIBARBO

Making your own rhubarb syrup means that you have to work for your cocktail, but the reward at the end is fantastic. We developed this when searching out seasonal recipes for the restaurant and rhubarb is one of the most quintessential things about a British summer. We had great fun turning it into a fantastic margarita.

50 ml/3½ tablespoons tequila
15 ml/1 tablespoon Rhubarb Syrup
15 ml/1 tablespoon agave syrup
25 ml/1½ tablespoons freshly
  squeezed lime juice

RHUBARB SYRUP
200–300 g/2–3 cups rhubarb,
  roughly chopped
3 whole cloves
200 g/1 cup caster/superfine
  sugar

SERVES 1

First make the rhubarb syrup. Simmer the rhubarb, cloves and sugar in a saucepan with 250 ml/1 cup of water over a low heat for about 15 minutes, until the rhubarb is soft and tender. Set aside to cool, then strain through a sieve for a beautiful, smooth syrup.

Combine all the cocktail ingredients in a shaker with a large scoop of ice. Shake hard for 8–10 seconds, then strain into a margarita glass with fresh ice.

A nice addition to make it even more summery is to muddle some strawberries in the shaker before adding the other ingredients and then shake as before.

This is another one that makes a fantastic non-alcoholic drink for all to enjoy. Simply trade out the tequila for cloudy apple juice and you are ready to go.

APPLE-RITA
MANZA-RITA

Out goes the vodka and in comes the tequila for our take on this 80s classic. The maple syrup and apple juice make a wonderful combination, cut with the heat of the tequila.

35 ml/⅛ cup Tequila Reposado
20 ml/1½ tablespoons apple juice
15 ml/1 tablespoon freshly
  squeezed lemon juice
15 ml/1 tablespoon maple syrup
1 dash of Angostura Bitters
2 thin apple slices
a slice of lemon

SERVES 1

Put the tequila, apple juice, lemon juice, maple syrup and bitters in a shaker and shake hard with a generous scoop of ice. Strain over fresh ice into a rocks glass.

Garnish with a straw and the apple and lemon slices.

GREEN JUICE WITH CACTUS
JUGO VERDE CON NOPAL

Chances are that you have never eaten cactus before and you are even less likely to have had it in a drink. Well, now is the time to start. The health benefits of the nopal leaf are fantastic with its spectacular vitamin count and many other nutritional qualities besides. They are not so easy to get hold of, but a quick online search should lead you to them.

1 stick of celery, plus a leaf
  to garnish
1 nopal leaf
1 fresh sprig of parsley
freshly squeezed juice from
  1 orange

SERVES 1

It is worth trying to get rid of as many of the sinewy threads of the celery as you can. Do this by gently snapping off the end and then pulling away the threads that hang on to it. The general rule is the fresher the celery, the fewer the threads.

Cut the celery into 4 pieces and slice the nopal leaf into 4–6 strips.

Blend all the ingredients together with 200 ml/generous ¾ cup of water for about 2 minutes until smooth. Pour into a glass and garnish with a celery leaf.

WHOLE LIME & MINT AGUA FRESCA
AGUA DE LIMÓN Y MENTA

We're not going to lie to you, this is one of those real 'love it or hate it' flavours. Using the whole lime, skin and all, gives this drink a unique flavour. We tried it out at Benito's and it was a straight 50:50 split between the lovers and the haters, with both sides passionate about the answer. We hope you are on the lovers' side!

6–8 large fresh mint leaves
3 limes, each cut into 4 pieces
130 g/⅔ cup caster or granulated
  sugar
500 g/1 lb 2 oz ice cubes

SERVES 4

Put the mint leaves, limes and sugar in a blender with 500 ml/2 cups of water and blend for about 2 minutes until well mixed.

Strain the mixture through a sieve into a jug/pitcher, add the ice and mix very well. Top up the jug/pitcher with cold water until it reaches 2 litres/8½ cups and stir thoroughly.

If you like your drink with some bubbles, substitute still for sparkling water at the topping-up stage.

COCONUT HORCHATA
HORCHATA DE COCO

The Mexican version of this traditional milkshake dates back many centuries. You will find many different flavours of this drink across all of Latin America and Spain. Here we have gone for the delicate flavours of coconut and cinnamon.

1 medium coconut
180 g/1 cup white rice
½ teaspoon ground cinnamon
25 g/2½ tablespoons caster or
   granulated sugar
625 ml/2⅔ cups whole milk
125 g/½ cup condensed milk

SERVES 4

Stick a metal skewer in one of the coconut eyes and drain the coconut water out (you can discard or better yet drink this separately as it is so good by itself).

Smash the drained coconut on a hard surface or floor to crack the shell, then open it up fully. Remove the white coconut from the shell.

Put the rice, cinnamon, sugar and 250 ml/ 1 cup of plain water in a blender and blend for 8-10 minutes. Add another 500 ml/2 cups of water, the whole milk and condensed milk and three-quarters of the coconut. Blend for another minute. Strain through a sieve to remove any little segments.

Use the remaining pieces of coconut either as a garnish on the rim of the glass or finely chopped and mixed into the drink. The drink should be served cold, so store in the refrigerator and serve over ice. Shake well before serving.

THICK WALNUT DRINK
ATOLE DE NUEZ

A traditional drink for Day of the Dead celebrations.

950 ml/4 cups whole milk
6 tablespoons maseca masa harina (fine
   yellow cornflour/maize)
100 g/1 cup walnut halves
¼ teaspoon ground cinnamon
4 tablespoons caster or granulated sugar

SERVES 4

Put 235 ml/1 cup milk into a glass and mix with the maseca and set aside. Blend together the walnuts and another 235 ml/1 cup of the milk for 2-3 minutes. Warm the remaining milk in a pan over a medium heat. Just before it boils, add the walnut mixture, maseca mixture and remaining ingredients. Simmer for 3-5 minutes, stirring continuously, until thick. Serve hot or as a cold drink over ice.

THICK CORN HOT CHOCOLATE
CHAMPURRADO DE LA TIA ROSA

This is for my sister, Rosa, who loves this drink.

1.2 litres/5 cups whole milk
8 tablespoons maseca masa harina (fine yellow
   cornflour/maize)
4 tablespoons chocolate sauce/syrup
4 tablespoons caster or granulated sugar
¼ teaspoon ground cinnamon

SERVES 4

Put 235 ml/1 cup milk into a glass and mix well with the maseca. Gently warm the remaining milk in a pan over a medium heat. Before it starts to boil, add the cornflour/cornstarch mixture and cook for 2-3 minutes, stirring. Add the remaining ingredients. Simmer for 5 minutes, stirring, until thick.

SUBSTITUTIONS There are a few speciality and tricky-to-find ingredients used in some recipes, so we thought they are worth a little explanation and have provided guidance on suitable substitutions.

• Sal Doña Nata: This is my mother's salt that she mines herself from the salt water springs near the family house in San Antonio Texcala. It is a beautiful ingredient with a delicate flavour and worth digging for, but Maldon Sea Salt is a good substitute.

• Ground avocado leaf powder: This is another family ingredient, this time farmed and produced by my brother Fernando. It has an aniseed flavour so if you can't get hold of these, star anise or fennel seeds work instead.

• Fresh tomatillos: Easy to find in the southern US, but very tricky in the UK, so tinned/canned ones will do (if using tinned, there is no need to peel and roast or boil as recipe methods have been written as if using fresh tomatillos). They are similar to tomatoes but with a unqiue tart flavour.

• Fresh chilli/chile de arbol: Bird's eye or Thai green chillies/chiles make a good substitute.

• Dried chilli/chile de arbol: About ½ teaspoon of dried, crushed chilli/chile will give the same degree of heat.

• Agave syrup: This is now pretty easy to get hold of in supermarkets. Honey and maple syrup will also give you the required sweetness but come with their own flavours, so be aware that using them as subsitutes will change the taste of the dish.

• 100% agave tequila: Don't kid yourself. Anything not labelled '100% agave tequila' is classified as mixto tequila, and mixto tequilas do not cut it for the flavour. In addition, your head will not thank you the next day if you go down the wrong path here!

INDEX

ACKNOWLEDGEMENTS

For both Felipe and I, Mexican food is all about sharing with family and friends; bringing people together and creating great memories. It has been part of Felipe's life from the beginning, and whilst I was not really exposed to it until I was in my twenties, I'm doing my best to catch up!

Much patience and support is required from family members when it comes to writing a book. Thanks to our wives, Siobhan and Kay Lee and to our kids, Ferran and Yasmin; and Penelope, Beatrice and Hazel. Our team at Benito's Hat, Walter Weinzettel, Felipe Pino and Carlos Duarte also deserve special mention for making our restaurants such a fantastic place to come to every day. They are the ones who keep the customers coming back, and we would be nothing without them.

Felipe would also like to thank his mum Doña Nata, after which his new restaurant in Cabos San Lucas, in Mexico is named, and his sister Rosa, whose recipes continue to be an inspiration. He would like to thank his friends Jessica Torres, for her help since he moved to Cabo San Lucas with his family, and Adalberto Martinez and Monica Zurita for their help, friendship and most of all for their belief in his new concept.